Beyond the Blurb
On Critics and Criticism

BOOKS BY
COW EYE PRESS

Cow Country (2015)
Adrian Jones Pearson

Beyond the Blurb: On Critics and Criticism (2016)
Daniel Green

Twelve Stories of Russia: A novel, I guess (2017)
A. J. Perry

Beyond the Blurb
On Critics and Criticism

Daniel Green

Beyond the Blurb: On Critics and Criticism

First published in the United States of America in 2016 by

COW EYE PRESS
1621 Central Avenue
Cheyenne, WY 82001
www.coweyepress.com

Copyright © 2016 by Daniel Green

All rights reserved. No part of this publication may be reproduced or transmitted in any form or by any means without written permission of the publisher.

For information about special discounts for bulk purchases, please contact editors@coweyepress.com.

Cover design by MAIN Design House

Publisher's Cataloging-in-Publication data
Names: Green, Daniel K., author.
Title: Beyond the blurb : on critics and criticism / Daniel Green.
Description: Includes bibliographical references. | Cheyenne, WY: Cow Eye Press, 2016.
Identifiers: ISBN 978-0-9909150-3-4 (pbk) | 978-0-9909150-4-1 (hardcover) | 978-0-9909150-5-8 (ebook) | LCCN 2016946765.
Subjects: LCSH: Literature--History and criticism. | Criticism--United States. | Critics--United States. | BISAC: LITERARY CRITICISM / General | LITERARY CRITICISM / American / General | LITERARY CRITICISM / Books & Reading.
Classification: LCC PN99.U5 G7 2016 | DDC 801/.95/0973

Contents

Introduction..........9

Part 1: Critical Issues..........17
    Close Reading • 18
    The Authority of Criticism • 21
    Aesthetic Autonomy • 29
    The Authority of Critics • 34
    Blogs and Alternative Literary Criticism • 39

Part 2: Critical Failures..........49
    James Wood • 50
    Christopher Hitchens • 65
    Morris Dickstein and Historical Criticism • 73
    Hershel Parker: Criticism vs. Scholarship • 79
    Postmodern Fiction and Academic Criticism • 84

Part 3: Critical Successes..........93
    Susan Sontag • 94
    Harold Bloom • 105
    Richard Poirer • 114
    William Gass • 120
    Michael Gorra's *Portrait of a Novel* and "In-Between"
        Criticism • 124
    David Winters's *Infinite Fictions* • 129
    S.D. Chrostowska's *Matches* • 134

Bibliography..........143

Acknowledgments..........149

INTRODUCTION

INTRODUCTION
ON CRITICS AND CRITICISM

I offer this selection of essays as a kind of cross-section of the views I have expressed over the last ten years or so about the goals and practice of literary criticism, views published on my own literary blog, *The Reading Experience*, as well as in various literary and book review journals. Place of publication played a large role in determining both the content and the form these essays took, since the blog essentially gave me the freedom to write as I pleased. As it turned out, what pleased me was to critically examine not just works of literature past and present but also the critics and critical methods whose influence helps to determine how "literature" is perceived and how literary works are made meaningful for diverse and at times disparate readers. All of the essays that follow are animated by this impulse to explicate the assumptions behind a practice referred to by a common name—"criticism"—but carried out in numerous and often quite conflicting ways.

The essays also of course reflect my own assumptions and preferences, and while certainly these are the assumptions and preferences that inform my work as a literary critic, in these considerations of critics and criticism I am making them explicit through commentary on other critics—although in the first section, titled "Critical Issues," I do directly address the more general questions confronted by all critics, in the process making my own thinking about "autonomy" or the efficacy of "close reading" expressly clear. Combined with the essays in the following two sections, on the failures and successes of particular critics, these discussions of what I take to be among the most important concerns confronting the literary critic ultimately present a philosophy of criticism that consistently returns to a few core tenets.

A literary work, whether in verse or prose, is worth taking seriously for its own sake, apart from any value it might have as the object of some other discourse or inquiry.

Although it is true that notions of "autonomy" that attribute to works of literature some kind of metaphysical separation from other forms of human communication cannot literally be sustained, much can be gained by acknowledging that artistic autonomy is a worthy ideal that in essence simply seeks to make room for a conception of literature that identifies poems and novels as first of all the source of aesthetic contemplation, verbal works of art, rather than conventional communication or just another form of "cultural discourse." Readers and critics are perfectly entitled to regard literary works in any way they want, of course, but to deliberately avoid initially engaging with them for their artistic value—the value with which their creators presumably most resolutely attempted to invest them—seems hardly in keeping with the animating purpose of literature as a form of expression. Perhaps readers need not seek out what Nabokov insisted on calling "aesthetic bliss" (although why not?), but that a work of literature might in fact produce such bliss would seem to be a fact about it that a literary critic, at any rate, should need to account for.

The meaning of a literary work consists of the experience of reading it, not in abstracted "themes" that signify what the work is "about."

A literary work is an arrangement of language designed to be perceived as such, not to impart sense as do the words of speech or ordinary prose. Some construe this assertion to effectively be a denial of meaning in fiction or poetry, but in fact it opens up the possibility of multiple, even infinite, meanings as the reader responds to the formal and stylistic effects the work's verbal processes make available, effects that can include the suggestion of meaning in its conventional sense—the writer is "saying something"—although exactly *what* is being said remains amorphous, indefinite. This meaning is fluid, provisional, enriching the reading experience, not replacing it with the inspection of texts for messages and ideas. If reading a work of literature is reduced to comprehending its theme, the experience itself has become at best a secondary goal, at worst, superfluous.

The goal of the literary critic should be to describe the work at hand as carefully as possible by scrutinizing his/her own experience of reading it as conscientiously as possible. Judgment is contingent upon description.

Even a 500-word book review, which is likely to accentuate evaluation, should convey the sense that the reviewer attended closely to the particular features of the work and has assessed its worth through honest reflection on the effects those features produce. Judgment without adequate description is useless as criticism, since it makes the critical act simply the expression of personal preference, the marshalling of suitable, if finally empty, terms of praise or censure.

The experience of reading is the experience of language.

In fiction and poetry we don't read "characters" or "setting" or "meter" or even "prose" or "verse." We read words shaped into sentences, figures, paragraphs, dialogue, stanzas, chapters, or, in the most synoptic application of language, made to suggest the presence of form, whether traditional narrative form or something more adventurous. My orientation to criticism was heavily influenced by New Criticism (something still being taught when I started graduate school), but what I took most from the New Critics was their "close reading" of the movements of language, so that I am inclined first of all to read fiction the way the New

INTRODUCTION

Critics read poetry, for the integrated effects of language, for the way the parts of the text make a whole and how the parts interrelate. Ultimately, of course, you can't avoid discussing such things as characters and point of view, but those are themselves the textual artifacts of language.

Criticism and scholarship are not the same thing.

Some of the critics discussed in this book, Richard Poirier and Harold Bloom, for example, could be called scholars. They are also critics. Both Poirier and Bloom are primarily engaged in the analysis and/or "appreciation" of particular literary works (or writers), although certainly the quality of their analysis is greatly enhanced by the great scholarly knowledge of literature both of them possess. Most of what is now called "academic criticism," however, is in fact scholarship, since its goal is not explication or evaluation but to create a body of knowledge about literature, or to locate works of literature in a specified context (a context that is itself usually of more interest to the critic than the work), whether that context is historical, political, cultural, or philosophical. I believe "criticism" should be reserved to describe the former activities, not the latter. This does not imply that criticism is more valuable than scholarship (or vice versa), more "literary" or more useful, merely that they are separate pursuits.

The greatest challenge to the efficacy of criticism is posed by what is called "experimental" literature, although this challenge also allows criticism to demonstrate its importance in mediating among writers, readers, and literature as a whole.

It is one thing for a critic to interpret the latest work of literary fiction or to help illuminate a work from the past that may have at one time been considered unconventional but now has become assimilated to critical norms, but when faced with a new work that does not conform to established norms, the critic's task becomes much harder, as well as more crucial. The critic must balance insight into the ways this new and seemingly unfamiliar work might actually maintain a connection to traditional practice with acknowledging what is truly fresh about it. The first of these responsibilities is just as important as the second, since originality can make an impression only when its point of departure from convention can be clearly discerned. Beyond just noting an original strategy or expression, the critic must also try to account for its success or failure in the work itself. Thus to fairly consider a work of innovative poetry or fiction, a literary critic must have creditable knowledge of literary history but must as well have sympathy for and sensitivity to writers and works that seemingly disrupt or deviate from that history. Finally such a critic is charged with initiating a process of reconciling the new and disruptive with a literary history that the new work, if it is successful, is destined to join.

※

*T*hese are, of course, *my* core beliefs about criticism, and certainly no one is obliged to share them or even to find them credible. They are the beliefs from which I wrote the essays in this book, and the beliefs that animate my own reviews of contemporary fiction. As should be clear enough, my views about criticism are closely tied to my views about literature. I value a kind of criticism that is capable of illuminating the sort of literary work I most admire, one that provokes, surprises, takes risks, but also satisfies aesthetically, in effect enlarging our perception of what can be considered aesthetic success.

I could have chosen other or different pieces to include in this book (probably illustrating to the point of tedium how extensively I do return to the basic principles I've identified), but what I have included is meant to elucidate an approach to criticism that takes literature seriously by granting it a fundamental integrity as a form of art, doesn't attempt to overshadow the literary work by subsuming it to another agenda or asserting the critic's own superiority of intellect or sensibility, but does also assume that criticism acquires authority through being rigorously attentive and articulating persuasive standards of analysis. Criticism in

INTRODUCTION

this form is both dependent on and independent of literature itself. Criticism arises because some readers feel a need to talk about the reading experience, because works of literature do not explain themselves; they leave the motives and principles of their own composition implicit. At its best, criticism can make these motives and principles explicit, without trespassing against that zone of the unspoken upon which literature depends.

Unless, of course, you are Jonathan Franzen, who believes that the work is a "contract" with its readers whose terms are thoroughly spelled out. Presumably this sort of work requires no critics. Mostly, though, such a notion just makes it clear why a writer like Franzen might not be worth reading in the first place.

1
CRITICAL ISSUES

PART 1

CRITICAL ISSUES

While certain core principles inform almost everything I write about literature and literary criticism, the essays included here seem to distil the "critical issues" in a particularly direct and relevant way. Some of them could be called reviews, while others are simply responses to something I had read, responses that I managed to shape into essays in which I endeavored to both describe the source's argument and make a coherent argument of my own. I'm not sure I would have ever attempted to write such essays as these were it not for the existence of *The Reading Experience*, of the "literary blog" in general.

The essays explore, sometimes more, sometimes less explicitly, the concerns that unify my approach to criticism, especially the practice of close reading, the nature of literature as an aesthetic form, and the role of criticism itself. While I do not argue explicitly in these essays that reflection on such issues might be especially important in the critical discussion of current/contemporary literature, nevertheless this is a necessary and underlying assumption. To the extent that the kind of focus on the "literary" qualities of poetry and fiction, that is, on those qualities that make them first of all works of art, for which I advocate has been dismissed as old-fashioned or superficial, new books are in danger of receiving only the most cursory notice, the most uncritical celebration or "takedown," otherwise left to fade into future obscurity.

Close Reading

In "A Critic's Manifesto" (*The New Yorker*, Aug 28, 2012), Daniel Mendelsohn contends that to be a critic requires "expertise, authority, and taste." He leaves out the most important attribute a critic should have: the ability to pay attention. In fact, without this one, the others Mendelsohn mentions are superfluous.

Any defensible judgment about a work of literature must arise from observable features on which the judgment is based and to which the critic can return. This is where the distinction between having an "opinion" about a text and being able to support that opinion is real. An opinion is only a provisional conclusion until it can be allied with and clarified by specific illustration from the work, until the critic can point to those particulars of the work that prompted the opinion. An unsupported opinion may or may not contain implicit but unstated illustration of this kind, but as long as it's unstated, it is not itself "criticism." Not everyone wants to be a critic, of course, but a book review, for example, can't really be taken seriously as criticism unless some text-based "evidence" is provided.

Providing such evidence requires that the critic pay attention. Close attention. This would involve, at minimum, noting, in fiction, such conventional elements as narrative structure (especially variations in narrative structure), character development (especially the writer's strategies for influencing our attitude toward characters), point of view, etc., but since fiction as a genre of literature is at its core the creation of illusions of such things as "character," "story," or "setting" through skillful manipulation of language, a critic needs ultimately to be able to focus on the writer's invocation of language, on the text as an artificial arrangement of words. Attempting to explicate a work of fiction by leaping first of all to plot or character or any other imposed device rather than considering the way such devices are conditioned by and embedded in language ignores the very medium through which literature exists, as if a work of fiction was really just like a movie aside from those pesky words. (Although film criticism certainly requires attention to the use of medium as well, in this case the manipulation of visual imagery.)

Being attentive to language does not mean picking out isolated passages of "fine writing" and making a fuss over them. More often than not, such purported fine writing is just the decorative cover for a work that otherwise does aspire to be a movie. Ultimately language is everything in a work of literature, and a critic needs to account for the way a writer marshals the resources of language to create all of the effects in that work. If, for example, "setting" seems to play an especially important role in a novel or story, a critic should be expected to notice the way the writer's prose works to make setting (again an illusion created with words) seem so prominent. To a significant extent, this means the critic needs to describe the work at hand as carefully as possible, or at least the work as experienced by the critic (and potentially the reader) paying close attention. Judgment, which critics such as Mendelsohn want to assign such an essential part in literary criticism, can only be justified, and ultimately taken seriously, if it is preceded by this kind of scrupulous description.

Absent the effort to give close attention to the tangible features of the literary work, to explain what the experience of reading that work is like, what Mendelsohn calls "expertise" is largely beside the point. If Mendelsohn means by using this term to suggest that someone possessing it is an "expert" reader in that he/she does indeed know how to pay close attention, then of course I agree with him, although it is not necessary to be "expert" in some credentialed way in order to exercise this expertise. If, as I suspect, Mendelsohn means that an authentic critic is one who can cite all the myriad books he/she has read, or has read all the right ones, or who possesses the appropriate academic pedigree, then this sort of expertise by itself is mostly meaningless. An amateur critic can read just as sensitively as a "professional" critic.

Indeed, the "authority" a critic can bring to the consideration of literary works can only come from the authority that the sensitivity and insight of any particular reading brings with it (although of course some critics can demonstrate over time a consistency of insight that gives that critic a kind of default authority). Unless the critic's work earns its authority, the sort of authority that comes from the supposed prestige of the publication in which that work appears or from some other external affiliation is just specious. Whenever someone like Mendelsohn (or Sir Peter Stothard, who recently opined about the "harm" blogging is doing to literature) complains about the loss of "authority" being suffered by literary criticism (or book reviewing), it always seems to me they're basically lamenting the loss of this latter, artificial, and self-assumed authority.

"Taste," of course, is the most subjective of the qualities Mendelsohn prizes in a critic, and the purported possession of it by some (critics) and its absence in others (too many readers) has long been used as justification for the implicit deference we are to pay to the "best" critics. At some level it is undeniably good for a critic to be able to discern the artful from the meretricious, but the notion of taste is also used, frequently I think, as the excuse for bringing attention to some books and writers and ignoring others, thus giving the former the tacitly official approval of the guardians of literary culture. When critics are presuming to act as such guardians, their "judgment" especially needs to be examined with skepticism, as this act of sorting (abetted by editors) can actually do harm to literary culture by excluding adventurous writers and elevating those more acceptable to the cultural mainstream. "Taste" is again something that can be validated only by the strength of the critic's descriptions and analysis. It shouldn't be assumed.

I do not say that Daniel Mendelsohn in particular is guilty of this offense or that he abuses the critic's privileges in the other ways I have described. I find most of his reviews to be perfectly sound, although I don't always agree with him. And I do agree with him when he says that the "serious critic ultimately loves his subject more than he loves his reader." The literary critic's primary allegiance should be to literature, to its continuation and continued vitality. If his/her "expertise" consists of ideas about how to effect this, if "authority" is something that helps to ensure it, if "taste" means being able to recognize when a writer or work is likely to contribute to the effort, then indeed the critic needs all of these qualities.

The Authority of Criticism

Ron Silliman begins *The New Sentence* (1987) with this unimpeachable claim:

> . . . if we look to that part of the world which is the poem, tracing the historical record of each critical attempt to articulate a poetics, a discursive account of what poetry might be, we find instead only metaphors, translations, tropes. That these models have a use should not be doubted—the relationships they bring to light, even when only casting shadows, can help guide our way through this terrain. Yet their value stands in direct relation to their provisionality, to the degree to which each paradigm is aware of itself as a translation of the real, inaccurate and incomplete.

Such a pragmatic perspective on the utility of "poetics" (of literary criticism in general) seems to me the most efficacious way of encouraging open-ended debate about all questions relating to a subject so thoroughly contingent as what properly constitutes the "literary" qualities of literature. (I especially like Silliman's reference to "that part of the world which is the poem," which correctly emphasizes that a poem is a phenomenon in the world, not a reflection on or of the world that somehow transcends or detours around the merely real. A text is an element of reality, not just an opportunity to discourse about it.) It is admirable that Silliman's first words warn against taking his own poetics as the last words on the subject, but as a critic he has firmly-held positions nonetheless, and they are positions that encourage readers to take sides.

Silliman next locates his approach as a critic by identifying himself with other poet-critics such as Pound, Olson, and Creeley, who were themselves situated "warily midway between the New Critics" and the "anti-intellectualism" that New Criticism provoked among "other sectors of 'New American' poetry." Although it seems to me that Silliman's criticism, both in this book and on his blog, has much in common with the close reading of the New Criticism, he is very harsh here in his comments about it, characterizing it as a "positivist" approach encompassing "an empiricist claim to transcendent (and trans-historical) truth." But the New Critics did not view poems as "empirical" evidence (the text) that would lead to a claim to "transcendent" truth (the critic's interpretation). This is, in fact, a wholly mistaken representation of the New Critics' project: New Criticism was "empirical" only in that it insisted readers attend to the perceptible structure and actual language of the text, and the only "transcendent truth" it implied was that reading a poem was not a search for transcendent truth. Indeed, the burden of New Criticism was exactly to convince readers to read rather than interrogate poems for their unitary "meaning."

Silliman makes his disdain for New Criticism (or at least the conception of "literature" he thinks it represents) even more blatant by comparing it to Stalinism:

> Necessarily...a poetics must be concerned with the process by which writing is organized politically into literature. It is particularly disturbing when, under the New Critics as well as Stalin, this transformation is posed and explained as though it were objective and not related directly to ongoing and fluid social struggles.

Certainly the New Critics were attempting an "objective" form of reading in that they believed a poem could be approached as a work of art with discernible features that could be identified by paying close attention—"dispassionate" is perhaps the term that might justifiably be used to characterize the attitude of the New Critics' ideal reader. And they surely did not have any interest in "ongoing and fluid social struggles" (at least where the analysis of literature is concerned) and would never have accepted that "a poetics must be concerned with the process by which writing is organized politically into literature." Silliman, of course, believes they were a part of such organizing nevertheless (a retrograde part), and in the first several essays in *The New Sentence* he undertakes to establish that indeed poetics is finally about politics, poetry "a form of action," presumably on behalf of those "social struggles."

These first few essays are aggressively Marxist in their declarations about the place of poetry. In "Disappearance of the Word, Appearance of the World," we are told that the transparency of language we encounter in much ordinary communication is part of "a greater transformation which has occurred over the past several centuries: the subjection of writing (and, through writing, language) to the social dynamics of capitalism."

> Words not only find themselves attached to commodities, they become commodities and, as such, take on the "mystical" and "mysterious character" Marx identified as the commodity fetish: torn from any tangible connection to their human makers, they appear instead as independent objects active in a universe of similar entities, a universe prior to, and outside, any agency by a perceiving Subject. A world whose inevitability invites acquiescence. Thus capitalism passes on its preferred reality through language itself to individual speakers. . . .

Because poetry "is not only the point of origin for all the language and narrative arts" but "returns us to the very social function of art as such," it is in the best position to combat this commodification. Indeed, "perhaps only due to its historical standing as the first of the language arts, poetry has yielded less to (and resisted more) this process of capitalist transformation." But it hasn't resisted enough. According to Silliman, "The social role of the poem places it in an important position to carry the class struggle for consciousness to the level of consciousness."

> By recognizing itself as the philosophy of practice in language, poetry can work to search out the preconditions of a liberated language within the existing social fact.

Despite the dogmatic tone of these passages, the underlying analysis of public language vs. literary language seems pretty cogent to me. Extending the analysis to fiction, Silliman notes that "the most complete expression" of the "invisibility" of language "is perhaps in the genre of fictional realism, although it is hardly less pervasive in the presumed objectivity of daily journalism or the hypotactic logic of normative expository style." Further, "it is the disappearance of the word that lies at the heart of the invention of the illusion of realism and the breakdown of gestural poetic form." That calls for simplicity of style and an emphasis on narrative—both in fiction and journalism—reflect an impatience with language as medium and the dominance of "message" is undoubtedly true, and the proposition that poetry especially represents an opportunity to "liberate" language from these constraints is one I can easily accept. But I fail to see why it is necessary to lay the blame for the crudity of public language specifically on capitalism, as opposed to the general human reluctance to pay attention to subtlety and nuance and willingness to accept the "preferred reality" of authority. Capitalism will get no propping up from me, but I can't see that it has uniquely invoked these human limitations.

Much of the logic of Silliman's poetics (as well as, ultimately, his own poetry) depends on the assumptions he brings about the "role of the reader in the determination of a poem's ideological content" ("The Political Economy of Poetry"). Silliman contends there is no "genuine" version of a poem, only those versions experienced by a particular audience at a particular time:

> What can be communicated through any literary production depends on which codes are shared with its audience. The potential contents of the text are only actualized according to their reception, which depends on the social composition of the receivers.

Again this is a defensible position, but again I fail to see that asserting reception is determined by "social composition" is to say anything very significant. At best it establishes that audiences and readers bring to the reception of poetry their life experiences and circumstances, but to make "social composition" into the kind of essentialized, metaphysical entity Marxists want it to be doesn't convert a mere sociological fact into a revelation. Similarly, to say that "context determines the actual, real-life consumption of the literary product, without which communication of a message (formal, substantive, ideological) cannot occur" seems to me little more than a truism, and belies the question whether "communication of a message" is the goal a poet ought to be setting for him/herself. It is the goal that Silliman is setting, although in his practice as a poet he does concentrate on the "formal" message, through which the substantive and ideological are finally expressed.

If in essays such as "Disappearance of the Word, Appearance of the World" and "The Political Economy of Poetry" Silliman contends that New Criticism (presumably Silliman wants New Criticism to stand in for other varieties of formalism as well) puts too much emphasis on author and text in determining the "potential content" of the work, in my opinion he compensates for this failing by in turn giving over too much of the opportunity to "actualize" content to individual readers. Silliman is right to insist that the reading experience must include the reader as part of the process—the reader must be up to the task of apprehending the aesthetic qualities of the text—but in his determination to make poetry the servant of Marxist social reform, Silliman, at least in these theoretical essays, wants the reader's attention so thoroughly directed at the "meaning" a poem might provide that whatever aesthetic effects might accompany it are at best an afterthought, at worst regressive cultural baggage that must be discarded.

Silliman is not advocating for a crudely propagandistic kind of poetry, reducible to polemic and explicit "statements." Indeed, the meaning he wants readers to get from poetry is conveyed indirectly, through its material formal and syntactic procedures. Silliman believes (or at least this is what the Silliman of these essays believed) that by frustrating the reader's ability to read "hypotactically" (via transparent language and explicit connections made between parts of a discourse), the reader could be made aware of the way in which capitalist culture maintains its dominance through hypotactic communication. Thus both Silliman's poetry and that which generally came to be called

"Language Poetry" employed instead a "paratactic" strategy, by which language refuses transparency and connections are denied (the former achieved mainly by the latter). The notion that parataxis might work to produce worthwhile poetry is far from outlandish, but while the disruption of expectations implied by Silliman's poetics could easily enough lead readers to a reconsideration of the assumptions behind conventional definitions of poetry, that this would in turn necessarily lead to increased skepticism about the machinations of capitalism is not a step in logic I can follow.

Silliman's most important exposition of his call for paratactic poetry, "The New Sentence," is largely free of Marxist rhetoric, and offers an account of what such a poetry might be like that even an apologist for New Criticism could take seriously. It is first of all a relatively straightforward and learned history of ideas about the sentence in both linguistics and literary criticism that demonstrates that the potential of the sentence as an autonomous unit of language has not really been appreciated. Silliman also discusses a few precursor poets, such as the French symbolists as well as Gertrude Stein, who point to this potential but don't finally fully realize it.

The "new sentence," for Silliman, is one that "has an interior poetic structure in addition to interior ordinary grammatical structure." The "poetic structure" of the poem derives from the poetic structure of the sentences, arranged into paragraphs, a device that "organizes the sentences" but is "a unit of quantity, not logic or argument." In combination, this approach "keeps the reader's attention at or very close to the level of language, that is, most often at the sentence level or below."

Thus the notion of "language poetry," which in effect forces the reader to attend to the poem's language as it comes, not in relation to the "syllogistic movement" we ordinarily expect between sentences and through the poem as a whole. It is ultimately a kind of prose poetry, and, according to Silliman "the new sentence is the first prose technique to identify the signifier [language itself]. . . as the locus of literary meaning. As such, it reverses the dynamics which have so long been associated with the tyranny of the signified [that to which the language refers], and is the first method capable of incorporating all the levels of language, both below the horizon of the sentence and above...."

Unless by "prose technique" Silliman means specifically techniques used in prose poetry, I really can't accept the assertion that the new sentence is "the first prose technique" to call attention to the signifier as an end in itself. Metafiction, anyone? However, the radical break with the inherited presumptions about what makes for "good poetry" is real enough. Still, as far as I can tell, there is nothing in Silliman's poetics that should alienate the most recalcitrant formalist (even a backsliding New Critic). One could easily conclude after reading "The New Sentence" that poets without the slightest interest in Marxist theory could adopt the new sentence as credo and produce potentially interesting poetry, a challenge to convention and ordinary ways of reading, yes, but not necessarily a challenge to poetry as an ongoing tradition. (Or to Western capitalism, although one could also imagine some readers making the connection between the two kinds of challenges that Silliman would like, pursuing the extra-literary implications of the strategy after engaging with it on a purely aesthetic level—in my opinion an appropriate reversal of Silliman's priorities that more suitably preserves the integrity of the literary text.)

Silliman's animus toward New Criticism is additionally unfortunate in that his own close readings of particular writers and their work are surely New Critical in spirit if not in fact. In *The New Sentence*, his essay on Jack Spicer, "Spicer's Language," is a very precise and ultimately very evocative analysis of one relatively brief Spicer poem (as well as, along the way, Ezra Pound's 84th Canto and a few additional Spicer passages). Granted, the burden of the essay is to show Spicer as an important influence on the new sentence, but I found it to be the best piece of commentary on Spicer's work I've read, typified by this sort of careful exposition:

> Spicer's poem is composed in one stanza, written in what are ostensibly sentences, with a surface conventionality that extends to the capitalization of the letters at the lefthand margin. We have already seen the amount of tension which

is set up in the first line ["This ocean, humiliating in its disguises"] by the irreducibility of the subject and its modifying clause to any single, simple envisionment. The leap to the second sentence is made before a verb occurs in the first. In being suppressed, this verb ("is"?) becomes yet another moment of an absent presence. And there are no less than five positions in the sentence which it could have taken, so that its absence (i.e., its presence) is not perceived at a single point, but instead floats freely, a syntactic equivalent of anxiety. Far more jolting to the reader, however, is that the two sentences to a degree that is nowhere possible in the Pound passage, appear to come from entirely different discourses.

The combination of detailed description and critical insight ("a syntactic equivalent of anxiety") is very satisfying, and here, as in similar readings posted on his blog, Silliman seems to me to exemplify a particularly scrupulous (and therefore all too rare) kind of literary criticism. While *The New Sentence* elucidates a poetics that affirms the active part played by the reader in locating the "potential content" of the poem, his critical readings nevertheless implicitly assert the importance of informed criticism, the existence of some readers who through skill with the "codes" always associated with attentive reading can help other readers overcome the limitations of their inherited codes and approach poetry in a more rewarding way.

It is indeed true there is no "universal" mode of poetry—no "normal poetry" from which anything else is an aberration—and it is also true that much conventional poetry, with its "normative syntax, classical metrics, and a deliberately recessive linebreak" requires "at the level of the reader's experience" only "passivity." (Although I can't accept the further complaint that this passivity means the reader "can only observe, incapable of action": observation is not what happens in our interaction with a text, only reading, which is itself a form of action.) Silliman's challenge to the universalist and passive conception of poetry is entirely well-justified and should not be dismissed. But it is literary criticism embodying universal intelligence that keeps the multifarious practices of poets from devolving into chaos, and Silliman's criticism participates in this stabilizing process. It is, after all, in critical writing such as *The New Sentence* and on his weblog that Silliman convincingly makes his case against universalist assumptions and passive reading. Yet the cogency of this case depends upon a reader willing to defer to a critic speaking in what can't be denied is a critical "voice" of manifest authority.

Aesthetic Autonomy

*J*ohanna Drucker sums up her argument in her book, *Sweet Dreams: Contemporary Art and Complicity* (2005), as follows:

> ...[T]he critical frameworks inherited from the avant-garde and passed through the academic discourses of current art history are constrained by the expectation of negativity. Fine art should not have to bear the burden of criticality nor can it assume superiority as if operating outside of the ideologies it has long presumed to critique. Fine art, artists, and critics exist within a condition of complicity with the institutions and values of contemporary culture.

According to Drucker, artists of the 2000s (representatives of which her book discusses in some detail), no longer see "complicity" with mass culture as an evil to be avoided. These artists use mass culture to create dynamic, visually arresting works the ultimate ambition of which is to be aesthetically pleasing. No requirement of "criticality" is necessary for ideological correctness: the purpose of art is to be aesthetic, and contemporary artists are exploiting the aesthetic possibilities of mass culture to create "fine art" that doesn't pretend to an inherent "superiority" over that culture. Complicity is okay, as is taking sensory pleasure in art.

I am ultimately fine with this argument, although it's unfortunate that a defense of aesthetic value in art has to in effect make common cause with mass culture in order to ensure that "art" survives as a viable endeavor to begin with. (It's the devil's bargain that's unfortunate, not popular culture, or at least particular productions of popular culture, some of which I enjoy just as much as the next fellow.) And why is it necessary to equate autonomy in art with a claim of "superiority"? Earlier in the book, Drucker tells us that the high modernist view of art as existing in a separate sphere actually did damage to the aesthetic claims of art:

> By appearing to be entirely aesthetic (its forms and expressions entirely contained in the visual appeal to the senses and lacking in any prescribed or circumscribed purpose), fine art sustains the concept of value as a notion by pretending to be autonomous. The "value" of a work of art is never to be accounted for in the costs of materials and labor or in the investments in production. Fine art appears to be far from the crass worlds of commerce and remote from the real world of factory production. Fine art distances itself from the systems that in turn exploit these myths to advantage. Art is not a shell game or a poker bluff, but an assertion of the symbolic basis of value production. . . .

It seems that Drucker is reciting the oft-told story of how modernist art took itself to be free of complicity, innocent of ulterior purpose, by "appearing to be entirely aesthetic" and "pretending to be autonomous" but really wasn't after all. It's an article of faith that academic criticism clings to like piranhas: art can't assert autonomy or singularity, can't carve out an aesthetic space beside the "crass worlds of commerce," because all expressions are socially or culturally or historically determined. Works of art can be studied alongside TV shows and pop albums because they're just as inevitably a part of culture as any other commodified object.

I say this is an article of faith because although it is true that all human beings creating works of art are subject to the prevailing assumptions of time and place, this does not seem to me to be a very profound observation. It amounts to saying that living artists are, well, alive rather than dead. (Or that deceased artists lived on this planet rather than on one in some adjacent solar system.) Yet it is held as an unassailable truth in post-New Critical academic criticism that literature must be historicized, that the unavoidable fact that writers put the fruits of their influences into circulation means that culture authors texts to the extent that the notion of aesthetic autonomy is just a misguided illusion.

But why does the fact that any artistic work can be seen to one degree or another as illustrative of cultural forces rule out the possibility it might also be granted a kind of autonomy? If your goal is to show that all cultural expressions are subject to the historical mediation demanded by a properly Marxist view of culture, you can certainly do so, and arguments about the "autonomy" of certain expressions that should be exempt from such mediation would correctly be dismissed as incoherent. But they would be incoherent only when considered from within this interpretive framework, which is being posited as the only acceptable way of making sense of works of art or literature.

However, if this particular way of making sense of artistic and cultural expression has the virtue of being true—albeit in the trivial sense I have indicated—it can hardly claim exclusive rights to truth since its own investment in it rests on the underlying assumption that truth is relative. If literary texts cannot claim to embody universal or unmediated or noncontingent truth because everything is an artifact of incidental human activity, I cannot see any logically disallowed reason why one such activity could not be the study of literary texts for their posited "literary" qualities conceived as separate from their status as cultural representations, congeries of historical forces, conduits of sociological information, or whatever else works of literature can be considered good for. To object that such an approach to literary study (or the study of any of the arts) presumes itself "outside of the ideologies" is either irrelevant—since all critical approaches must scramble to the "outside" in order to speak authoritatively about the "inside"—or just wrong. The "autonomy" game does not presuppose itself outside the rules of relativism; it simply solicits recognition as one game among the others. "Pretending to be autonomous" is good enough for those who think this particular aesthetic game yields interesting insights. "Appearing to be aesthetic" is, in fact, to be aesthetic.

Thus the real question at issue is not whether autonomy is a valid concept in art/literary criticism but which concepts are to be accorded primacy in academic criticism. If the notion of the "autonomous object" is accompanied by close and accurate reading that results in a coherent account of a text or work of art, it can hardly be dismissed as fallacious. It can be assigned a lesser significance in the critical hierarchy, deemed less "serious" in an environment in which the merely literary and the merely aesthetic are identified with a dandy-ish formalism and can be marginalized safely enough while real scholars get on with the business of interpreting history, explaining culture, and intervening in politics. It can be made the scapegoat for all the shortcomings of the previous generation's critical assumptions and duly assigned its own historicized place in the critical, and curricular, past. In the struggle for dominance in that small part of academe originally (if reluctantly) set aside for "literature," the proposition that poems, stories, and novels are best regarded as wholly unlike other, more transparently discursive verbal texts, self-enclosed, formally intricate, autonomous, and that the critic's job is to advance ways of reading such texts that enhance the reader's experience of them, has clearly lost out. It is unlikely to make a comeback, although periodic efforts like Drucker's to defend aesthetic pleasure will no doubt still persist.

Although it does seem to me that a debate about terminology, about the conventionality of the critical lexicon, is still in order: When the powers-that-be in literary study want to show they have not entirely abandoned the old critical order, they like to point out that much current academic criticism arises from what they want to still call "close reading." But this term has become so overstretched through misuse that, at best, it now merely means "paying attention" and at worse means "interrogating" the text vigorously enough that you finally do find there what you wanted to find. "Close reading" for the New Critics was a reading adjusted to the contours of the text, a reading that seeks to conform itself to the demands made by the text itself, and doesn't demand that the text conform to the critic's preconceptions. It does so by, indeed, assuming the work's autonomy.

"Literary criticism" is still identified as the task undertaken by academics who study and write about literature. But academic criticism often seems to have little use for the "literary" as a subject of inquiry except when it can be shown to be illusory, or elitist, or a prop supporting various evil hegemonies. Since it is clear enough that many academic critics would rather be engaged in cultural criticism, ideological criticism, or sociological analysis—anything but the lowly explication of literary texts—perhaps the term "literary criticism" could be turned back to those who do have an interest in exploring, even appreciating the possibilities of the literary when considered as an autonomous practice. I'm really not sure why cultural studies scholars and historicists would want to hold on to the designation, anyway.

Then there are terms such as those used by Drucker: "negativity" and "complicity." By the first, Drucker seems to mean the incorporation of images, motifs, and sensibilities from mass culture only to "subvert" these references by using them to implicitly critique the insipidity of mass culture. This has been a common response to the encroachment of mass culture on high art, and Drucker is right to suggest that sometimes high art simply borrows from popular culture and that such borrowing is not always an attempt by the artist or the writer to "say something" about culture. That this move attributing "criticality" to works is so familiar only reinforces (for me) the extent to which criticism of art and literature has become wholly fixated on the something said at the expense of the forms of saying (and how form itself mutates straightforward "saying"), but I'm not sure why she needs to use "complicity" as a description of the act of avoiding negativity.

The term only reinforces the notion that artists and writers must be judged by the sociopolitical consequences of their work. Drucker wants it to be acceptable for them to refuse the "burden of criticality," but to be inevitably "complicit" with cultural practices and attitudes expressing sometimes dubious "values" can't help but suggest there is a lack of integrity in the art work found complicit, a lack of purity that makes art and literature questionable allies in the fight against temporal Power.

For me, that they are weapons of questionable efficacy in this ideological skirmish is the mark of their most indispensable value. In their excesses and frequent ungainliness, their refusal to submit to the expectations of ordinary discourse, works of art and literature manifest an a-temporal power that compels succeeding viewers and readers to consider them anew (sometimes to enlist them in ideological skirmishes), to regard them as representations informed by their origins in historical circumstance but not bound by them, however culturally complicit they ultimately must be. If this is not quite metaphysical "autonomy," it's also not an illusion.

The Authority of Critics

John Carey's *What Good Are the Arts?* (2005) is a very strange book. Its first half seeks to demonstrate that art doesn't really exist and that, if it does, it doesn't do anyone any good. The second half essentially ignores the case that Carey has just made and asserts that art does indeed exist after all and does some people quite a lot of good.

The first half is actually the more interesting and lively part of the book. Here he surveys all the various efforts made to define art and finds them wanting, concluding that "Anything can be a work of art. What makes it a work of art is that someone thinks of it as a work of art." The relativist in me wants to concede that ultimately this is true: no Platonic definition of art that thoroughly delineates those properties inherent to art and that marks it off from all those other phenomena that are "not art" exists. We wouldn't want one even if we could get it. Rogue artists who confabulate our notions of what art is and isn't are always going to come along, and we should be grateful for them, even encourage them. "Art" is, finally, whatever succeeding generations of human beings determine it to be.

On the other hand, when we all put on our logical thinking caps, we know that if "anything" is art, nothing is. There are just "things" that provide us with enjoyment, pleasure, instruction, or whatever we want to call whatever it is we get from these things. One could plausibly enough adopt this view (the pragmatist in me thinks it wouldn't ultimately matter because it wouldn't really affect our sense of the value of what it is we do "get" from these things), but Carey himself finally doesn't want to go this far. He wants to retain the word "art," even if it does reduce art objects to those "things" someone, somewhere, thinks to call art. (Later in the book Carey tries to raise "art" back up to a more dignified status by stressing its utilitarian applications, but for it to have such applications it surely does have to exist in the first place, or those using it won't exactly know what they're applying.)

Thus Carey is able to argue further that "art" as it is celebrated by its snootier adherents doesn't have the morally elevating qualities they want to claim for it. No plausible evidence exists that art makes us better people. Most of the rhetoric used to pronounce on its spiritual qualities Carey incisively, and rightly, points out is so much bluster and metaphysical cant. If we can't provide specific scientific descriptions of the effect art actually does have on us (and Carey maintains that we can't) then better to remain silent than to make grandiose assertions about its "spiritual authenticity" or its ability to evoke "a peculiar emotion" that is "independent of time and place," as Clive Bell had it. And not only is the "religion of art" rhetorically bankrupt but it in fact "makes people worse, because it encourages contempt for those considered inartistic."

Curiously, then, Carey winds up not so much rejecting the ethical function of high art but affirming its ethical dimension: Too much attention to the wonders of art and too much discussion of those wonders only work to make us bad people. That art turns out to be morally enervating rather than elevating doesn't make it any less "moral" in its implications.

Carey's inability to rid himself of the very assumptions he wants to decry runs throughout the chapter charging arts enthusiasts with turning it into religion. Such enthusiasts apparently are wrong not so much in thinking that art might have beneficial effects but in failing to spread those effects around widely enough: "Turning art into religion often carries with it the assumption that there is a higher morality of art, distinct from conventional morality." The religion of art "devalues, by comparison with itself, ordinary life and ordinary people." Furthermore, it is the focus on the appreciation of, rather than participation in, the arts, that keeps it floating above the outstretched arms of those "ordinary people" who might after all be made into better people if they were to experience the joy of art for themselves. As evidenced by various studies Carey cites, feelings of powerlessness might be alleviated (resulting in a decrease of violence), self-esteem might be raised, and an epidemic of depression might be halted. Thus, "Another thing we should do is to switch the aim of research in the arts to finding out not what critics think about this or that artwork—which is necessarily of limited and personal interest—but how art has affected and changed other people's lives."

Notwithstanding that Carey's contentions in this chapter essentially contradict everything he's said before—art can't be "anything" or there would be nothing specific to apply in the kinds of arts programs whose beneficent effects he lauds, and there would be no reason to enlist the arts at all in such programs if they can't change lives—they don't even count for much in Carey's own ultimate valuation of "art" in the second section of the book, "The Case for Literature." It turns out that Carey's brief on behalf of participatory art was only a kind of gesture toward a quasi-Deweyan program of "making art," good for bashing the swells and the necessarily limited efforts of critics, perhaps, but not really a serious defense of an alternative to Art. Literature, it would seem, actually is art, and its primary effects are to be located in the secondary act of reading. (I agree that they are, but in the context of Carey's overall argument about the subjectivity of standards, it nevertheless brings the critic back into prominence, as the reader who proves to be especially attentive.)

Carey titles his first chapter on the subject "Literature and Critical Intelligence," but his initial argument seems to place "critical intelligence" in literature rather than the reader: "The first claim I would make is that, unlike the other arts, [literature] can criticize itself." It "shows itself more powerful and self-aware than any other art." Perhaps this is true, but if so, it very nearly belies Carey's larger point that art—even the premier art of literature—doesn't have any particular, objective value. (Yes, Carey assures us that his valuation is indeed his unavoidably subjective own, but still. Carey's very attempt to offer concrete reasons for literature's superiority seems to assume at least an objective method of assessing its superiority.) "More powerful" suggests that works of literature do have some experiential qualities that can be measured. Furthermore, Carey believes that literature "is the only art capable of reasoning" and that "only literature can moralize." (He seems to be using "moralize" in a sense that makes it a good thing, something like a "critique" of human behavior.) Swift and Johnson are presented as authors whose works illustrate these capacities.

Carey appears to have adopted some variation on the otherwise presumably "elitist" French-theoretical idea that language, not writers, create texts, since it is "literature" that reasons and moralizes. If he means instead to say that individual authors such as Swift are moralists, this is just another way of describing their particular interests. It says nothing about literature as "art" per se. According to the terms of Carey's discussion, it is literature that moralizes, literature that reasons.

I confess I find this idea absurd in the extreme, essentially insane. Carey is hearing voices speak through literary texts that no critic or reader with a decent respect for fiction or poetry as distinctive modes of discourse would hear in such an unmediated way. Moreover, Carey himself apparently doesn't really accept these formulations. The final chapter of *What Good Are the Arts?* tries to make a case for literature based on its characteristic "indistinctness."

> All written texts require interpretation and are, to that extent, indistinct. But with Shakespeare something new happened. An enormous influx of figurative writing transformed his language—an epidemic of metaphor and simile that spread through all its tissues. . . So when writing is dense with metaphor and simile. . .the imagination has to keep fitting things together that rational thought would keep apart. It has, that is, to keep ingeniously fabricating distinctness—or whatever approximation to distinctness it decides to settle for—out of indistinctness. . . .

As it happens, I thoroughly agree with all of this. "Indistinctness" is a perfectly good name for that evasive quality in works of literature that sets them apart from straightforwardly discursive forms of writing, that in the most intensive way requires we really read the text before us. But I don't see how at the same time we are grappling with the "indistinctness" of literature we can also comfortably accede to its "reasoning"—after all, "the imagination has to keep fitting things together that rational thought would keep apart"—or its "moralizing." Either literature "says something" about morality or politics or ideas in the kind of readily accessible way Carey's discussion of it implies, or it is "indistinct" and thus all of its putative messages are unavoidably ambiguous when they're not just hopelessly garbled.

Carey wants to have it both ways: it is because literature can "communicate" more effectively and it can also remain "indistinct" in the manner common to all the arts that it is ultimately the most valuable of the arts. Perhaps this is just the consequence of the fact that literature emerges from language as its medium and that language is inevitably burdened with "meaning" (although it is also the consequence of a failure to consistently distinguish between the use of language for meaning and the use of language for aesthetic effect), but it nevertheless results in the most crippling contradiction in a book full of contradictions. Literature can't both produce an indistinctness that every reader makes distinct in his/her own way (or leaves it indistinct) and make moral and rational claims that are presumably universal in their appeal.

As far as I can tell, Carey seems to have written this book in order to upbraid the likes of critic Geoffrey Hartman, who, according to Carey, believes "the experience he gets from high art is better than that others get from the mass media." Since there is no way of establishing that high-art lovers do obtain a "better" experience therefrom, or even of establishing what "better" might mean, all defenses of high art are simply expressions of elitism dressed up in patronizing rhetoric.

But what if the experience of art does contribute to human improvement? Not because art's moralizing or "spiritual" qualities directly lead to social change or self-actualization, but because close consideration of art enhances our ability to have fulfilling experiences? Because complex works of art encourage us to pay attention in a way that does not direct it into pre-existing channels or entirely cut off the very possibility of sustained, fully-engrossed attention by settling for the superficial or the sanctimonious. Even if there is no way of measuring the quality of experiences of this sort vs. the quality of the "anything" someone might want art to be, who really thinks that anything will do? Near the end of the book, Carey offers a sop to art-lovers: "That the arts are enjoyable to those who enjoy them is a fact that it may seem I have not emphasized enough in this book. If I have not done so, it is partly because it is obvious, and partly because being enjoyable does not distinguish the arts from a vast range of other human activities." But what if it's why the arts are enjoyable "to those who enjoy them" that's important? Not because it confers some special honor on their declared tastes but because the enjoyment comes from having one's powers of apprehension challenged?

And why can't the objects of this particular kind of enjoyment be called "art" by those who care about it? Why does John Carey want them to stop calling it that, unless they also stipulate that "anything" can be art if claiming otherwise makes the "inartistic" feel bad? It's finally only Carey who seems to believe that "art" must have a metaphysically-fastened, all-encompassing definition, or else there's nothing.

❧

Blogs and Alternative Literary Criticism

In 1974, Richard Kostelanetz published a book called *The End of Intelligent Writing: Literary Politics in America*. Amplifying arguments Kostelanetz had been making throughout the 1960s and early 1970s, the book posits that "the end of intelligent writing" is being hastened by two obstacles making it difficult for such writing to reach an audience: control of the reviewing/critical media by a self-perpetuating group of like-minded editors and writers, and the blinkered perspective of publishing companies obsessed with finding best-sellers and committed to their current practices simply because they are what have always been done.

Kostelanetz calls the cabal controlling critical discourse the "New York mob," but this mob is essentially comprised of the group of critics arising in the 1950s and early 1960s that has come to be called the "New York Intellectuals." This collection of critics—mostly Jewish and mostly politically radical (although anti-communist) were associated with the creation and flourishing of *The Partisan Review*, *Commentary*, *Dissent*, and, somewhat later, *The New York Review of Books*. The New York critics were notable for bringing literature into "intellectual" debates, but their predominant approach to literature (almost exclusively fiction) was intensely political and sociological. They disdained an "aestheticist" approach to literary criticism (their betes noires were the New Critics), and while some of them championed the great modernist writers of the immediately preceding generation, the appeal of modernism was not its formal or stylistic innovations but the way in which it provided insight into the "modern condition" of alienation and uncertainty. (For some of these critics, modernist writing provided them a way to forget their previous allegiances to Communism and its kind of "engaged" writing.)

Kostelanetz excoriates the New York Intellectuals (especially Norman Podhoretz, Irving Howe, and Jason Epstein) both for their aesthetic conservatism and their chokehold on what was published as "serious" criticism through their control of the most highly regarded magazines and their ability to reward and promote their acolytes. As the agenda-setters, they influenced critical discourse to the extent that challenges to their critical principles (and to their liberal anti-communism) were summarily dismissed when not simply ignored.

Kostelanetz's case against the big publishers is somewhat less conspiratorial:

> The larger American trade publishers—the literary-industrial complex—responded to the new prosperity by developing a consuming interest in the big killing. Individual firms differ, to be sure, but certain practices and assumptions have become almost pervasive. Anything offering the promise of

huge success now commands a comparably huge advance, which is often several times larger than what was available only a decade before. Authors of previous best-sellers are particularly favored, partly because the rule of precedent suggests that their next book will continue to attract a large audience, but also because such stars radiate an "aura" that seduces publishers as well as readers.

Not only are literary agents more adept at scoring extravagant contracts for hyper-commercial properties, but editors make their reputations not upon the solidity and breadth of their commitments, but upon a few fortuitous choices—"big books," as they are called. . .Oscar Dystel, the president of Bantam Books, speaks for his colleagues in judging that, "There is no disastrous situation in publishing which cannot be saved by the publication of one really big best-seller.". . . .

The "rule of precedent" states that what has happened in the past must guide future decisions. One might say that a similar such rule governs the publication of criticism and reviews as Kostelanetz describes it. Only the kind of criticism that had previously been published in the "mob" periodicals would continue to be published. "Serious" or "highbrow" criticism was defined as what appeared in those periodicals, and any other possible approach was marginalized as less than serious, even in (perhaps especially in) publications not otherwise directly affiliated with the New York intellectuals themselves. Just as in publishing the rule of precedent results in the same old kinds of books getting published, in criticism it creates an environment in which the same old critics proceeding under in-common assumptions are those allowed a public voice.

The particulars of Kostelanetz's indictment are dated (he names names throughout), but its general outline remains relevant. Indeed, Kostenlanetz's description of the practices of book editors and publishers might even still apply directly. Publishers continue to pursue the "big killing," authors with a track record of financial success are still preferred, editors hope for that "fortuitous" find that will "take off." The rule of precedent continues to determine what titles will appear on the seasonal lists. If anything, these methods (to the extent they could be called thought-out methods) are being even more desperately employed now than in the 1970s. Perhaps only the proliferation of independent presses has allowed "intelligent writing" to persist, since the big publishers appear not to consider at all the value of making such writing available, which arguably some publishers in the past did, out of a sense of obligation to literature. There are no indications that anyone in today's "book business" feels such an obligation. The notion that they ought to no doubt mostly seems absurd.

The more interesting question is if something like the situation Kostenlanetz describes in relation to literary criticism still obtains. Whether or not Kostelanetz's specific critique of the *Partisan Review/Commentary* critics is a fair one (and it does uncomfortably suggest that The Jews Control Everything), it seems to me unquestionably true that a critical establishment hostile to formally innovative fiction and inclined to view fiction primarily as cultural symptomology (and to ignore poetry altogether) did dominate book reviewing and generalist criticism after World War II, and in my opinion this critical orientation persists, if in a somewhat diluted and decentered form. Magazine and book review editors are doubtless as guilty of cronyism as Kostelanetz contends the New York critics were, but cronyism is probably unavoidable in what is essentially a closed system in which self-appointed "gatekeepers" feel it is necessary, given the limited space available, to carefully monitor access to the gate. Kostelanetz maintains that the New York critics were able to bring attention and esteem to the writers they designated "important," particularly Saul Bellow, whose reputation as a "great" writer was earned mostly through the relentless efforts of these critics to proclaim him such. Can anyone look at the hype surrounding, say, Jonathan Franzen and deny that something similar is at work?

Is it merely a coincidence that when one goes through the weekend book review sections of the most prominent newspapers one finds the same books covered? Sometimes the critical verdict is positive, sometimes negative, but that this particular book—usually a work of conventional psychological realism and/or written by a "name" author—was deemed significant enough to warrant review in the first place is what counts (including for whatever future attention and sales the book gets, even if an individual review points thumb down). By whatever combination of publisher PR, reflexive deference to name recognition, an underlying herd mentality, and sincere conviction that the books selected truly do represent the best American fiction currently has to offer, editors (and reviewers) mutually work to set and reinforce an agenda that determines which writers and books deserve consideration. As much now as in 1974, new and experimental writers need not apply, unless the writer has the right pedigree (respected writing program, previous publication in eminent journals), the right publisher, has already achieved notoriety in some other way, or has written a book so unusual it has some interest as a curiosity. The influences on book reviewing appear to be such that what emerges when considering print book reviewing as a whole is a collective disdain for work that introduces novelty or uncertainty into the process of judgment.

I aspired to become an academic critic precisely because so much general interest criticism was focused on the "mushy middle" of literary fiction and avoided the books I was most interested in reading. Academic journals were much more likely to feature experimental and unconventional writers (some journals concentrated exclusively on such writers) and gave them more than the cursory treatment afforded by most book reviews. Academic criticism no longer manifests these virtues, however. It is as agenda-ridden as literary journalism, although its agenda emphasizes a different kind of propriety, the propriety of political and cultural analysis (in its way similar to the kind of analysis favored by the New York Intellectuals). And while academic journals continue to offer longer and more sustained commentary, this commentary is more concerned with context—historical, culture, theoretical—than with the text, the latter serving only to illuminate the former. Academic criticism of contemporary fiction no longer provides a more rigorous, expansive, open-minded alternative to the popular reviewing media. For text-based criticism, the general interest book review is what we're stuck with.

At one time I held out hope that the "literary weblog" would provide a plausible alternative to print book reviewing. I still think that, in theory and potential, blogs could still be perfectly good sources of serious literary criticism. There is nothing in the nature of the cyber medium that precludes the blog from being the publishing vehicle for serious writing of any kind. If serious critics, facing the likely demise of newspaper and magazine reviewing in the not distant future, turn to the cyber/blogosphere as an available substitute, literary criticism will flourish well enough. Such book reviewing sites as *The Quarterly Conversation* and *Full Stop* have already demonstrated that online reviewing can be just as credible as print reviewing, in many cases going far beyond, both in length and in critical heft, what is offered in all but the most studious general interest print publications. They are also much more likely to cover experimental and translated works and books from independent presses, which are at best sporadically reviewed in mainstream print book review sections. Unfortunately, it cannot at this point be said that the literary blog has validated hopes it might sustain a form of general interest criticism that could replace, perhaps even surpass, what is left of print criticism. There are indeed some very good literary blogs offering worthwhile criticism, but on the whole the literary blogosphere has become largely an echo chamber for book business gossip, pseudo-literary trivia, and the establishment perspective. Literary blogs have become not an alternative to the established critical order but part and parcel of it.

Those blogs now calling themselves "book blogs" in particular have pledged themselves to this order. Mostly devoted to superficial appraisals of potboilers and best-sellers, these blogs actively seek to be conduits of publishing propaganda (in the guise of "promoting" books). They have apparently become the most popular type of "literary" blog, and if "book blog" eventually becomes the name applied mostly to such weblogs, the future of literary criticism online is bleak indeed. But even those still self-identifying as "literary blogs" have settled in to an overly cozy relationship with both publishers and the print reviewing media. (Many of the bloggers have themselves sought out reviewing opportunities in the print media, as if the ultimate purpose of creating a literary blog was after all to attract enough attention to catch on as a newspaper reviewer.) While in general one does get from literary blogs a fuller sense of the diversity of fiction available to readers (more emphasis on independent presses) than from the print book reviews, too many of the posts devoted to specific books are discussions of the newest and hottest from mainstream publishers. Much time is spent obsessing over lists of various inane kinds (the Top 10____), and in preoccupation with prizes, the dispensing of which apparently substitutes for criticism absent the real thing,

Literary blogs are (unwittingly, I hope) abetting the capitalist imperative to get out "product" as quickly as possible. New books appear, are duly noted, presumably consumed, and then we're on to the next one. While sometimes lit bloggers consider an older title, it's usually by an already established author or a "classic" of one sort or another. Little time is spent considering more recent books that might not have gotten enough attention, or assessing a writer's work as a whole. Once the book has passed its "sell by" date, nothing else is heard of it and every book is considered in isolation, as a piece of literary news competing for its 15 seconds. The more potential readers come to assume that this is the main function of lit blogs, the less likely it is that the literary blogosphere will have any lasting importance. Literary blogs might let you know who reviewed what in the *New York Times*, but that *The New York Times* might not be the best place to go for intelligent writing about books is not something they'll have the authority to suggest.

2
CRITICAL FAILURES

PART 2
CRITICAL FAILURES

Since the most direct way to underscore problems with current preconceptions of criticism is to identify them in practice, I here present essays on prominent critics who seem to me to fall short of fulfilling criticism's promise to provide insight and enlightenment because of a needlessly constricted approach. My analysis of the flaws in the methods favored by these critics is not intended to deny their very real accomplishments (especially with Morris Dickstein and Hershel Parker) but to point out where an overly narrow conception of criticism's function leads to misguided judgments or even an implicit depreciation of the promise of literature itself.

The longest piece in this section is the first on James Wood, in which I critique his approach to criticism at length. (Some might say excessive length.) Wood seems to me a particularly pernicious influence on contemporary criticism, not because he is a "bad" critic per se but because he has used his undeniable skills in close reading to perpetuate a regressive and sectarian view of "how fiction works," as the title of his most influential book has it. Wood is so universally praised as a critic that I have felt especially provoked to delineate what seem to me his very obvious biases and to expose the real harm they do to fiction's potential by discouraging readers from expecting it to surprise or challenge orthodoxy, to attempt a redefinition of the form.

James Wood

*T*he limitations of James Wood's *How Fiction Works* become evident in just its first few pages. In his "Introduction," Wood tells us that although he admires the critics Victor Shklovsky and Roland Barthes, among their deficiencies was their failure to write as if they expected "to be read and comprehended by any kind of common reader," a mistake that Wood himself presumably will not make. ("Mindful of the common reader," he writes a little later, "I have tried to reduce what Joyce calls 'the true scholastic stink' to bearable levels.") But exactly who, or what, is the "common reader"? Is it the reader who keeps up on all the latest mystery novels? Who these days prefers memoir to fiction? Who might be led to read literary fiction if it could be made rather less literary? More to the point, does any kind of common reader turn to highbrow French or Russian literary critics for help with their reading strategies in the first place?

Even if we were to concede the existence of large numbers of enthusiastic readers just waiting for the right literary critic to come along and illuminate the deeper mysteries of fiction for them, Wood's book surely would not perform this task. *How Fiction Works* is no more free of a constricted perspective and of "specialized" discourse than *A Theory of Prose* or *S/Z*. What would a "common" reader make of this passage, from the chapter called "A Brief History of Consciousness"?

> Under the new dispensation of the invisible audience, the novel becomes the great analyst of unconscious motive, since the character is released from having to voice his motives: the reader becomes the hermeneut, looking between the lines for the actual motive. On the other hand, the absence of a visible audience seems to make the ordinary man seek an audience, in ways that would have seemed grotesque to lordly figures like the Macbeths. Many of the characters in *Crime and Punishment* seem compelled to act out horrid

pantomimes and melodramas, in which they stage a version of themselves, for effect. [King] David and Macbeth were men of action—you might say they were naturally dramatic (they knew who their audiences were); Raskolnikov is unnaturally theatrical, or better still, histrionic: he seeks attention, and he is desperately unstable and unauthentic, hiding at one moment, confessing at another, proud in one scene, self-abasing in the next. In the novel, we can see the self better than any literary form has yet allowed; but it is not going too far to say that the self is driven mad by being so invisibly scrutinized.

It isn't so much the use of the formal critical term "hermeneut" that would cause the untutored reader to pause in puzzlement over this paragraph (although such a reader almost certainly would have no idea what the term means, even with the brief and partial illustration that follows it). The whole notion that the reader needs to be analyzing characters in novels for "unconscious motives" would likely seem peculiar, even for those with some vague understanding of Freud. Why would we want to regard characters in a novel as if they were actual people, people with minds and motives and a "consciousness"? What do we need with motive when we have violence and insanity? Equally, the idea that Raskolnikov is play-acting for the reader, is both "theatrical" and "histrionic," has to seem just as strange, except to the extent that one might wish these scenes to be over quickly so the real action might begin. To suggest that the real action occurs precisely in the character's "histrionics," that in a novel like *Crime and Punishment* "we can see the self better than any literary form has yet allowed," is probably only to confirm that literary criticism has little to offer the common reader after all, as it seems so plainly antithetical to the "motive" a truly common reader—one who reads fiction not to "see the self" but to escape the self—brings to the act of reading.

And the common reader would not necessarily be wrong in dismissing Wood's analysis of the "invisible audience" and its hermeneutical scrutiny of literary character, for reasons that go beyond an initial resistance to pretentious language and an opaque reading strategy. While it is arguably productive to read Dostoevsky for his revelation of "unconscious motive"—arguable because it is just as sensible to forego engaging with Raskolnikov and his tedious mental machinations and emotional hysterics—Wood doesn't intend his examination of *Crime and Punishment* and other of Dostoevsky's books to apply only to his fiction. For Wood, the opportunity to access the "mind" of a fictional character is the primary reward of reading, the representation of a mind at work the principal goal of fiction writing. Wood's account of "how fiction works" is prescriptive, not descriptive: he wants to convince his common readers that the way of reading he presents in his book is the one proper way of reading and that the kind of fiction that most directly satisfies the specified readerly requirements is the only kind really worthy of our attention.

Wood next sets out in his introduction a list of "essential questions" he asserts his book will be answering:

> ...Is realism real? How do we define a successful metaphor? What is a character? When do we recognize a brilliant use of detail in fiction? What is point of view, and how does it work? What is imaginative sympathy? Why does fiction move us...?

The answer to the first question is, of course, "yes," and from this contention all else in Wood's critical construction follows. The purpose of fiction, as Wood will ultimately put it, is to set down "life on the page," albeit with the "highest artistry." The separate chapters of *How Fiction Works* are aimed at convincing us that this artistry consists of judicious use of metaphors (avoiding the kind of "writing over" of character committed by vulgar stylists such as John Updike and David Foster Wallace), creation of characters whose "life on the page" is presumably to be located on that part of the page where "mind" is found, the supply of moderate description that doesn't indulge in an "over-aesthetic" appreciation of sensory details, and the near-exclusive use of third-person point of view and the "free indirect style," which is itself the novelist's most essential strategy for creating "imaginative sympathy" and producing fiction that will "move us."

Perhaps Wood's recipe for a ready-made fiction seems only reasonable, an unexceptional set of ingredients likely to result in a recognizably "serious" novel of fine writing and "psychological realism." And should one feel that this sort of novel is the right and proper sort of thing novelists ought to be writing, then probably nothing beyond Wood's account of the essentials of good practice needs to be said. But for those of us who think that Wood's description of "how fiction works" is but one possible (and highly tendentious) description, that despite Wood's occasional citation of a still-living writer and his lip service to the notion that the novel "always wriggles out of the rules thrown around it," his account is mostly backward-looking, an examination of what has been done, rather than forward-looking, a discussion of fiction that emphasizes what still might be done. The message that "any kind of common reader" is likely to take from his book is that the art of fiction is now settled, all of the possible aesthetic innovations the form might offer already achieved. If you want to read the best that fiction has to offer, Wood's book clearly enough implies, stick with the line of Anglo-European fiction extending from Henry James to Henry Green. If you want to be an esteemed writer, do what Dostoevsky does, what D.H. Lawrence does, what Virginia Woolf and Saul Bellow do.

Wood is currently the most well-regarded generalist literary critic in the English-speaking literary world, and it is discouraging to say the least that such a figure uses his influence to conduct a rearguard action against the forces of change in literary practice, against those who, like William Gass (Wood's bête noire in this book), want to transform our perception of fiction as the effort to depict "people" and "life" to one that can encompass that goal (with many provisos) but can also capture the reader's attention in other ways, ways more responsive to the possibilities of fiction as imaginative manipulation of language and form. Wood makes his case for realism always within a context in which it is endangered by postmodernists and other stylistically immoderate writers who don't appreciate its subtleties and are tearing fiction away from its proper relationship to "the world." (American writers seem particularly guilty of this offense, as the brief references Wood makes to such writers as John Barth, Thomas Pynchon, and

Don De Lillo are mostly derogatory, while no mention at all is made of important post-World War II American writers such as Stanley Elkin, John Hawkes, Donald Barthelme, Rikki Ducornet, or Kathy Acker, all of whom no doubt violate one or another of Wood's critical strictures.) Thus, in the final paragraph of his introduction, Wood informs us that "fiction is both artifice and verisimilitude" and that he will "give the most detailed accounts of the technique of that artifice…in order to reconnect that technique to the world."

Wood, as well as many other literary critics concerned about the alleged loss of "the world" in fiction, seems to think that this is the most pressing difference between the kind of life-reproducing realism he advocates and the fiction of writers who don't understand or respect it—those writers are withdrawing from the world, are more interested in the "artifice" than in the "connection" that must be made to the world of experience. Now, if making such a connection means merely that the novelist's artifice is fashioned out of accumulated experience—that is, through what is learned by being alive—then a connection between art and world is always implicit in a work of fiction. But Wood means in his formulation to suggest "connection" between the work and the world outside the work as if that world were being attached to the words of the text by an umbilical cord of reference. For whatever reason, extreme partisans of literary realism such as James Wood want to regard a novel, which is ultimately a prose composition, an artful arrangement of words, as somehow containing "the world," rendering people, places, and things not just metaphorically—or as Gass puts it, as "pretended mode[s] of referring,"—but as real "objects of perception."

This underlying allegiance to realism as the conduit to life, however, is in Wood's case secondary to the higher-order reality of human consciousness, gaining access to which is Wood's most dedicated mission as a reader of fiction. To that end, the first chapter of *How Fiction Works* is devoted to an anatomy of point of view, quickly settling on the free indirect style of third-person narration as the strategy most conducive to the task of representing consciousness. Wood succinctly and effectively describes the free indirect style—"The narrative seems to float away from the novelist and take on the properties of the character, who now seems to 'own' the words. The writer is free to inflect the reported thought, to bend it round the character's own words"—but in declaring its effects to be the most satisfying the novel can ever produce he is foreclosing the possibility novels might in the future develop in new and surprising directions, directions taken, for example, by such recent novels as Tom McCarthy's *Remainder* or Zachary Mason's *The Lost Books of the Odyssey*. And here again Wood does not merely intend to suggest that novelists can sometimes perform a little trick that persuades us to suspend our disbelief and pretend along with the author that we're actually exploring the "mind" of a character, a character we also agree to consider a "person," at least for the duration of the narrative in front of us. "Mind" as trope or conceit, as an illusion the writer creates to get on with the writing, simply won't do. "Mind" in fiction must be as "real" as any other phenomenon of the world; "life on the page" must be a mental life, with which the greatest writers allow us to "merge."

Ultimately the most disconcerting thing about *How Fiction Works*, and about James Wood's criticism in general, is that while Wood on the one hand expresses near-reverence for the virtues of fiction, the terms in which he judges the value of fiction as a literary form implicitly disparage it. He doesn't want to let fiction be fiction. Instead, he asks that it provide some combination of psychological analysis, metaphysics, and moral instruction, and assumes that novelists are in some way qualified to offer these services. He abjures them to avoid "aestheticism" (too much art) and to instead be respectful of "life." As he puts it in his book's conclusion:

> The true writer, that free servant of life, is one who must always be acting as if life were a category beyond anything the novel had yet grasped; as if life itself were always on the verge of becoming conventional.

To the extent it is fully clear what this sentence is supposed to mean, it seems to posit that the novel exists to record life, to "grasp" at it even though life will elude the grasp (or at least the novelist must always fear it will). Fiction is to be measured by the justice it does to life.

There is another view of what fiction can accomplish, one that does not make it subservient to an agenda of fidelity to "the real." In this view, what continues to elude the novel as a form is the limit of its own potential for innovation. In this view, life is always already conventional, and a novel exists not as a reproduction of reality but as an addition to it, a supplement. And in this view, a work of fiction is measured by the justice it does to the aesthetic possibilities of the form, possibilities that surely exceed the arbitrary boundaries James Wood wants to enforce. Readers of *How Fiction Works* should keep in mind that, even if it is true that "The house of fiction has many windows, but only two or three doors," the door being opened here is still not the only one available.

In his discussion of the free indirect mode in *How Fiction Works*, Wood asserts that "we're stuck with third- and first-person narration," the free indirect version of the first—or what Henry James called "third-person central consciousness"—being for Wood the most effective way to give us access to "Mind" in fiction. Perhaps ultimately Wood's real skill in this book is the way in which he convinces his readers to overlook the fact that such an assertion is certainly debatable, indeed taken literally quite obviously wrong. We're not really stuck with third- and first-person narrators of the conventional kind, but certainly James Wood is quite content with these alternatives, especially since he can so quickly establish the limitations of all but the free indirect method for fulfilling fiction's highest aspirations. If we were to add to Wood's brief on behalf of this narrative strategy his historical analysis in *The Irresponsible Self* that privileges a certain kind of moral-centered "comedy" (which he also more accurately describes as "a kind of tragicomic stoicism"), we can see that Wood's critical project works to first isolate and then elevate a particular kind of modern novel, loosely the comedy of manners, at which English writers have proven especially adept (although Wood also extends his attention to certain European writers who also favor psychological depth and "tragicomic stoicism"). The comedy of manners has certainly played an important part in the development of fiction (and many very good writers have participated in the genre), but admirers of James Wood's book reviews should realize that the judgments he makes as a reviewer are rooted in his preference for this sort of fiction and should remember he has devoted most of two books to the attempt to critically justify the view that it represents not just a significant achievement in the art of the novel but is in fact the settled form in which that art can be realized, that the literary history of the novel in effect comes to an end with its ascension.

Not every book Wood praises as a reviewer is necessarily a comedy of manners, as his collection of reviews, *The Fun Stuff*, shows, but almost all of them are ultimately found to be "realistic" in the way they reveal "Mind" at work and/or they can be taken as "comic" in Wood's formulation. (Because this concept of comedy is essentially a religious one—it is a "comedy of forgiveness," Wood tells us—a novel like Marilyn Robinson's *Gilead* is an especially direct recent illustration.) What might seem to be an exception to Wood's predominating terms of analysis, a work such as Lydia Davis's *Collected Stories* (which Wood praises highly), can turn out to be perfectly compatible with them, as long as you look at the work in the right way. Davis's enigmatic, experimental stories would not suggest themselves as something that would appeal to James Wood, since he is known for prominently dismissing experimental, innovative, or reputedly postmodern fiction, often harshly ("hysterical realism" being perhaps his most famous coinage for dispatching such fiction to the fringes of respectable critical discourse), but it turns out you can really ignore the alternative aesthetic purposes enigma and ellipsis might be serving in Davis's fiction and reduce her stories to a collective autobiographical expression, the soliloquies of a "composite" narrator that, unsurprisingly, allows us access to that narrator's inner life:

> In more conventional fiction ... the reader is allowed to overhear the thoughts of other people. In Davis's soliloquizing work, a narrator is often overhearing herself, and we are then allowed to hear their painful and funny self-overhearing.

What makes Davis's fiction "unconventional" is the complexity with which it gives us access to Mind, encompassing secondary and tertiary levels of "overhearing." We witness "a mind spinning like a fly," thus, presumably, justifying the discontinuities and extreme compression all readers will most immediately encounter in Davis's stories. It is of course the way these strategies challenge the established conception of "story" that is really unconventional in her stories, but Wood manages to discount what is truly unusual in Lydia Davis's work to extract the usual sort of value he wants to find in fiction. In fairness to Wood, Davis's stories are first-person narratives, so the analysis here is not one that buttresses the free indirect style, nor does Wood's review of Norman Rush's *Mortals*, which similarly lauds Rush's use of a first-person narrator to achieve psychological complexity. But in each case the end of the analysis is to draw out the psychological complexity, the means by which the writer produces it praised to the extent it makes the revelation of psychological depth visible. When Wood says that some novels allow us to experience "the thoughts of other people," he betrays his ultimate assumption that fiction is valuable because it helps us understand human behavior at its source in mental processes, an accomplishment that is essentially a moral one because to understand is to "forgive" the weaknesses we all share. But fiction does not present us with either "people" or "thoughts." It presents us with words artfully disposed to invoke the illusion of such things as people and their thoughts.

I do not think this is a trivial distinction. It seems to me a fundamental difference between regarding works of literature as sources of wisdom or special insight (which surely most novelists do not manifest to any greater degree than anyone else), as aids to understanding, and regarding it as the use of language to create literary art. Certainly there is room for disagreement about what is considered the "proper" purpose of literature. Some readers (and some critics) want "content" from the fiction or poetry they read, indeed want works of literature to "say something" about human experience as depicted either through the behavior of individual characters or through their interactions with social and cultural forces. It is also true that such "saying" can be direct or indirect, as James Wood probably believes is the case in those works he praises for their psychological acuity. Such fiction in a sense unwittingly, through the formal and stylistic choices the author has made, reveals the operations of Mind. In remaining faithful to the perceptions and the cast of thought projected on the characters they have created, writers of fiction use the resources of fiction to illuminate the nature of consciousness. In either case, however, these readers and critics are turning to fiction for what it is "about," although not necessarily in the most reductive sense in which this means preoccupation with "the story." Most of the novels James Wood approves most enthusiastically, in fact, are notably short on plot, which only gets in the way of providing depth in characterization.

Wood no doubt would also say that in focusing our attention on this quality of fiction he is not ignoring the "art" it exhibits. The burden of analysis in most of his reviews, he might say, is on patiently showing how the writer's aesthetic devices make the particular sort of character depth found in the work possible. Indeed, Wood has been called the "greatest living critic" precisely because of his reputed ability to engage in this kind of close and patient reading. But while it is true that Wood appeals to the particulars of the text more than most mainstream reviewers (although in my opinion, some of his reviews indulge more in plot summary than close analysis), his readings do not usually attempt to give a full account of the text's aesthetic features, preferring to concentrate on those that contribute to the achievement of psychological realism. Even when he is presumably not constrained by the conventions of the periodical book review, as in his essay on Richard Yates, Wood gives a minimum of detailed textual analysis, reverting instead to a great deal of biographical framing, plot summary, and generalized observation about Yates's realism. Wood does offer some close reading of the tangible features of *Revolutionary Road*:

> Yates's novel is both traditional and radical. Its traditionalism can be felt in the way it so delightedly flourishes the artisanal virtues of structure and finish. The prose is nicely alert and poised. . . . The book's form is a solid delight of symmetry and repetition . . .

These are potentially interesting insights into the formal and stylistic attributes of *Revolutionary Road*, but while Wood offers a couple of brief illustrations to substantiate such claims, they don't go very far in elucidating the aesthetic character of the novel. We are left with vague formulations ("delightedly flourishes the artisanal virtues") and subjective judgment (nicely alert and poised") in place of fuller and more rigorous description. Wood follows up these remarks with a paragraph asserting that *Revolutionary Road* "is essentially a novel all about artifice, and thus about its own artifice." The first part of this statement is perhaps obvious enough that it does not require much additional support. The second part is not (it certainly doesn't immediately follow upon the first) and, while it is a provocative comment that could substantively affect our response to the novel if true, Wood does not at all establish it is true except at the most superficial level: "Frank's theatricality is a form of fiction making, after all." Finally, Wood's essay does almost nothing to validate the notion that *Revolutionary Road* is both traditional and radical, which is a shame, because it might, in fact, be valid.

In an essay on Edmund Wilson, Wood finds that Wilson's predispositions as a critic "frequently lead him away from an aesthetic account of a work toward biographical speculation and cultural instruction." This is an accurate enough assessment of Wilson's limitations (although *Axel's Castle* remains one of the best contemporaneous books on modernism, precisely because Wilson was sensitive to its aesthetic challenges and was able to trace their roots in 19th century symbolism), but while Wood is usually more focused on aesthetic elements than Wilson was, surely his description of Wilson's critical predilections apply to Wood himself. If Wood's reviews of new books do not often introduce biographical information, among the essays included in *The Fun Stuff*, those on Yates, George Orwell, V.S. Naipaul, and Thomas Hardy lean heavily on biographical exposition (as does the essay on Wilson), as if when the writer's work becomes historical most of what needs to be said concerns the writer's life instead (or that now the work can be more correctly explicated in the context of the life). In essays like these, Wood assumes more the role of literary historian than a purveyor of "close textual reading," the conclusion Wood reaches about Wilson. Wood is less directly concerned with "cultural instruction" than Wilson indeed arguably was, but it is nevertheless more accurate to call Wood a moral critical than a formalist interested in close reading for its own sake. For Wood, the effort to penetrate the veil of consciousness and behold the mind at work is a moral one, for both writer and reader.

For the writer, the emphasis on the inner life of characters is itself an implicitly moral act, at least when the writer is able to fully and successfully exploit the inherent capacity of fiction to reveal the inner life. It is moral because, as Wood says of Jane Austen's fiction, such an act allows characters and their behavior to be "gradually comprehended and finally forgiven" ("Comedy and the Irresponsible Self"). It is the writer's success in exploiting this capacity that constitutes the "art" of the work, but the art is in the service of the moral goal. For the reader, the novelist's skill in achieving this sort of compelling psychological realism allows us to inhabit a perspective other than our own, to become aware of "the thoughts of other people." If Wood doesn't exactly attribute a didactic moral purpose to fiction, he certainly does suggest throughout his reviews and critical essays, as well as in *How Fiction Works*, that the moral effects of our encounter with other "minds" are what make fiction valuable to us as a form or genre of writing. And if Wood doesn't much dwell on the "cultural" issues or implications of the fiction he considers, his selection of works or writers to assess and the consistent return to his core concerns related to narrative strategy and the portrayal of character signal a clear desire to "instruct" readers how to read fiction for what it most importantly has to offer.

This is not to claim that Wood never engages in more wide-ranging aesthetic analysis, nor that his aesthetic judgments are always suspect because of his partisan motives. His ability to evaluate aesthetic worth perceptively is perhaps most conspicuously on display when he renders an all-out negative judgment, as in his review of Paul Auster's *Invisible*. Wood is unsparing in his criticisms of Auster's skills as a stylist, maintaining that Auster "does nothing with cliche except use it," but even Auster's staunchest defenders could hardly claim that vivid writing is one of his strengths. Likewise, Wood incisively critiques Auster's awkward status somewhere between realist and postmodernist:

> One reads Auster's novels very fast, because they are lucidly written, because the grammar of the prose is the grammar of the most familiar realism. . . . There are no semantic obstacles, lexical difficulties, or syntactical challenges. The books fairly hum along. But Auster is not a realist writer, of course. Or rather, his local narrative procedures are indeed uninterestingly realist, while his larger narrative games are anti-realist or surrealist, which is a fancy way of saying his sentences and paragraphs are quite conventional, and obey the laws of physics and chemistry, and his larger plots are almost always ridiculous.

To call the plots "ridiculous" rather than use some other, less obviously derogatory term to describe their "surrealism" ("outlandish") is perhaps excessive, but again it is hard to cavil with Wood's conclusion that "what is problematic is the gravity and emotional logic that Auster seems to want to extract from the 'realist' side of his stories, making it harder to credit the postmodern disassembly" Auster also applies to his narratives.

Yet it has always seemed to me that it is precisely the odd disjunction between Auster's conventional, even trite, mode of narration and the weird situations and plot turns to be found in the narratives that makes Auster's best fiction both distinctive and compelling. Predictably enough, Wood has very little sympathy for such a phenomenon, since no way of accounting for the effect Auster's fiction has on receptive readers will turn Auster into a psychological realist. But Wood's problem with Auster, his legitimate analysis of the writer's shortcomings notwithstanding, seems to me a problem he has with many American writers, who emerge from a literary history much different from that which produced the English comedy of manners or the European/Dostoyevskian psychological novel. Wood seems to know little about this history, or at least gives no indication he would be inclined to acknowledge the alternative literary values the writers in this tradition embody. He concentrates his appraisal of Auster's fiction on the conflict between Auster's realist strategies and his postmodern inclinations, but if Auster is a postmodernist, he is one of the sort anticipated by writers such as Hawthorne and Melville, writers of "romance" whose plots could be described as at least as "ridiculous" as Auster's and many of whose works (especially Hawthorne's) could be interpreted as proto-metafictions.

Hawthorne and Melville were emphatically not psychological realists. (The power of the portrayal of Ahab in Moby-Dick comes from the fact we do not know what's going on "inside his head"; we have only Ishmael's reports of his behavior to go on.) But even the American realists of the late 19th century and early 20th centuries (Henry James being a significant exception) were not realists of the kind valorized by James Wood. Their work still relies heavily on plot, emphasizes setting in its external, palpable details, and remains "outside" the characters it portrays, following their actions but rarely restricting the narrative to what these characters themselves perceive. This mode of realism continues well into the 20th century in modern naturalists such as Steinbeck and Richard Wright. It doesn't seem likely Hemingway would rank high in Wood's pantheon, nor the later neorealists and minimalists influenced by Hemingway. Flannery O'Connor's bleak allegories contain little in the way of either psychological subtlety (again, the creepiness of many of her characters arises from our lack of access to their "thinking") or of the comedy of forgiveness. One imagines that Wood's critique of Auster (along with earlier critiques of Don DeLillo and David Foster Wallace) is a critical stand-in for a broader critique of postmodernism itself, but since Wood has not directly written about any of the older, foundational postmodernists, we can only infer that the problems he has with these more currently prominent writers are the same sort of problems he would have with William Gass, John Barth, Robert Coover, Gilbert Sorrentino, etc. That Wood rarely if ever even mentions such writers and their work strongly suggests he doesn't want to remind his readers of their challenge to his unequivocal declarations on behalf of psychological realism and the free indirect style, would rather not engage in the sustained analysis and argument it would take to make the case that American postmodern fiction as exemplified by these writers, as well as the literary tradition from which they emerge, should not be included as genuine examples of "how fiction works" as well.

Readers less interested in American fiction probably find Wood's frequent reviews of European fiction most satisfying, as well as a welcome exception to the general neglect of translation in the mainstream book-reviewing media, and indeed Wood may be at his best when reviewing such work (as well as British fiction). In *The Fun Stuff*, his reviews of Laszlo Krasznahorkai and Ismail Kadare, as well as the reviews of Kazuo Ishiguro and Alan Hollinghurst, perform the very useful service the best reviews can offer, which is to, on the one hand, convince us that a writer with whom we are unfamiliar is one we need to read, or, on the other, suggest to us through a judicious reading that our doubts about such a writer seem well-founded. In these reviews, that Wood privileges a particular mode or strategy matters less because the writers considered clearly do work in that mode and they are (or seem) especially accomplished at advancing its potential. If Wood made less grand claims on behalf of realism centered in subjective states of consciousness, acknowledging that it is one mode among others the writer of fiction might choose (and if others made less grand claims about Wood as the greatest critic of our time), I, for one, would likely find myself less resistant to his critical authority and more likely simply to appreciate his strengths as a reader of a certain kind of psychologically inflected fiction.

The two finest essays in *The Fun Stuff* are the first and the last, and neither is about literature. Readers might find both somewhat surprising, at odds with Wood's image as a rather stuffy defender of elite cultural values. In the title essay, Wood celebrates Keith Moon (and implicitly the music of the Who). Not only might it seem curious that James Wood admires a rock 'n' roll drummer (although he tells us in the essay that he was himself an aspiring drummer), but it seems even more unlikely that he would admire such a wild, seemingly undisciplined drummer as Keith Moon. However, Wood does a very good job of showing why Moon's apparent lack of discipline was really just the most visible manifestation of considerable, if unorthodox, skill. It is certainly refreshing to find Wood celebrating the unorthodox, even if it is in a musician rather than a writer, but his enthusiasm for Keith Moon's unconventional talent is palpably sincere and in fact rather moving. The book's concluding essay, "Packing My Father-In-Law's Library," ultimately takes a contrarian view of the urge to accumulate books and of the notion that a personal library is a meaningful clue to its possessor's life and character. Wood helps to move his late father-in-law's books and concludes that "the more time I spent with my father-in-law's books, the more profoundly they seemed not to be revealing but hiding him, like some word-wreathed, untranslatable mausoleum." Wood ultimately confronts the "rather stupid materiality" of these left-behind books, making them simply burdens on those forced to dispose of them, and he resolves "not to leave behind such burdens for my children after my death."

Neither the generosity toward the unconventional nor the iconoclasm displayed in these two essays are much in evidence in Wood's writing on literature, unfortunately. Paradoxically, they make reading *The Fun Stuff* more rewarding, but also cast his limitations as a literary critic in a harsher light.

Christopher Hitchens

"*Is* there a more relevant (and readable) literary critic than Christopher Hitchens?" asked the *Independent* in 2003. The immediate occasion provoking this rhetorical question (to which the implicit answer was, of course, "no") was the paperback publication of Hitchens's *Unacknowledged Legislation*, but the notion that Hitchens has proven himself an astute critic of literature has become remarkably widespread. If anything, his reputation as, specifically, a literary critic has only grown in the years following the events of 9/11/01 and Hitchens's own transformation into a "contrarian" of the neoconservative variety, as if those readers who had previously admired Hitchens for his political convictions have in response to his apparent apostasy nevertheless attempted to salvage something of their previous esteem by seizing on what seems to be his non-political writing about literature.

But very little of Hitchens's criticism is actually non-political. In almost all cases—book reviews, polemical essays, critical introductions—his focus is rather relentlessly on "writers in the public sphere," as the subtitle of *Unacknowledged Legislation* has it. This does not mean that he invariably turns to writers who in some way validate his own political allegiances; indeed, one of the more admirable characteristics of Hitchens's approach to literature is his willingness to take seriously even writers whose political views must be (or must have been) anathema to him—Kipling, or Wodehouse, or Evelyn Waugh. To this extent Hitchens clearly enough knows that to privilege politics above all is to trivialize literature. However, whether because his background is not in literary criticism per se, or because he does consider the political consequences of a writer's work (more often, the legacy of a writer's political ideas and attitudes) to be what is finally most serious about that work, Hitchens very seldom examines a "literary" writer except to foreground politics or political history, and usually only takes up writers whose work lends itself quite obviously to such discussion in the first place.

If in fact Hitchens is able to discuss works of literature as worthy of attention only in their political-historical context, he is certainly not alone among contemporary critics. It is bad enough that academic literary criticism has become almost entirely a species of political rhetoric and barely concealed agitation, but much so-called "general interest" criticism as well seems to proceed on the assumption that books and writers are to be taken seriously only if they appear to raise "issues" of sociopolitical interest, or at least can be read as conforming to highly politicized assumptions about what works of literature are good for. Some magazines, on both the left (*The Nation, The New York Review of Books*) and the right (*The National Review, Commentary*) rarely even review fiction or poetry unless it has some manifest political relevance, while others (*The New Republic, The Weekly Standard*) just as infrequently review such literary works without judging them according to "standards" that are difficult to separate from the political preferences for which such publications are known. Indeed, it has become something of a common practice for all of these magazines, which are most likely to publish lengthier, more closely considered literary criticism beyond what is to be found in newspaper book reviews, to regard contemporary literature simply as material, sometimes ammunition, sometimes a target, to be employed in the ongoing culture war.

Which is not to deny that some writers do produce novels and poems that are expressions of political sentiment, or that explore political ideas, or that use literary form as a rhetorical disguise for sociological analysis and political proclamation. (And there are also, of course, writers who have produced stirring political poems and otherwise aesthetically sound novels that happen to take on politically-charged subjects.) Nor is it to deny that political criticism has any useful function to perform in the larger project of modern literary criticism. Ultimately works of literature are valuable to us as readers precisely because they allow us access from so many different angles of approach, make themselves available for interpretation and appraisal rather than simply "communicate" ideas or information. Calling attention to the political implications of a particular literary work is not in itself objectionable, but the primary job of someone who wants to claim title to "literary critic" ought to be, if the word "literary" is to retain its ostensible meaning, to assess a work of literature as literature—its formal characteristics, its stylistic accomplishments, the whole range of its thematic concerns, all of the features to be found in a poem or story or novel that contribute to the distinctive experience reading works of literature can and should be.

Political criticism is thus subsequent to literary criticism. It is not identical with it. Political context may provide an ancillary (but not for that reason negligible) avenue of interpretation, but it is not in itself "literary" criticism if the literary qualities of the work at hand have not been established and to a certain extent given precedence. The political implications of a work of fiction or poetry are entirely legitimate subjects of discussion, but to focus on them to the effective exclusion of other possible sources of meaning only marks such discussion as political discourse rather than literary critique. (The position I am taking here is perhaps reminiscent of that taken by the "New Critics" in their response to the highly politicized criticism of the 1930s. However, while

I admire the New Critics for their insights about the integrity of the literary work and about the way in which the act of reading literature must be an active and open process, I am not advocating a resuscitation of New Criticism in its doctrinaire form. I do believe that these insights were valid, and ought to guide even non-academic criticism that explicitly identifies its subject to be "literature.")

Hitchens himself does claim that it is literature that intrigues him, that, as he puts it in the introduction to *Love, Poverty, and War* (2004), "there is a gold standard, and . . . literature establishes and maintains it." Yet even this latest book, in which Hitchens elaborates further of his "love of literature" that he "had begun to resolve, after the end of the cold war and some other wars, to try to withdraw from politics as such, and spend more time with the sort of words that hold their value," exhibits the habitual strategies Hitchens the critic brings to bear in his consideration of the work of poets and novelists: his almost exclusive focus on British and Irish writers, mostly from the first half of the twentieth century; his tendency not only to confine his interest to political subjects and to the most politically relevant writings by the authors in question, but to the political attitudes and opinions these authors can be seen to represent; more often than not, his inclination to focus even more narrowly on biographical and historical information, partly in order to carry out the political analysis he favors, partly because the sorting of such information seems to be Hitchens's fundamental assumption about what criticism is supposed to do.

To some extent, all of these assumptions are most effectively and convincingly embodied in *Unacknowledged Legislation*. Although, writes Hitchens in the Foreword to the book, he doesn't "engage with political writers" per se, he does examine "writers encountering politics or public life." This is straightforward enough, and he further specifies what he is trying to accomplish in the book by asserting that he has "attempted to show how some artists have almost involuntarily committed great political writing." That Hitchens doesn't really succeed in this ambition is not entirely the result of a flaw in the stated goal itself. A book compiled of separately published essays written for a variety of occasions is, at best, likely to advance a consistent thesis incompletely. Some essays will more directly illustrate the thesis—which is, almost literally, an afterthought, a good idea in retrospect—while others seem irredeemably tangential. The essays in *Unacknowledged Legislation* are united by Hitchens's interest in writers and "public life," but the unity seems tenuous, to say the least.

The biggest problem with the book's announced focus, however, is precisely in the terms in which it is stated. Just how "involuntarily" have the writers discussed in the book "committed" political writing? Enough to cover over the conceptual chasm that separates "artists" from polemicists? Or, more specifically, that separates art from politics, if either or both are to be more than words of such permeable meaning that one can be merged into the other at the critic's convenience? Perhaps Hitchens believes that in claiming these writers "involuntarily committed great political writing" he is preserving a safe space for "art" in the writing of fiction and poetry, but one could ask why he so plainly prefers the involuntary actions of these literary artists to their more relevant voluntary achievements.

Perhaps it is only understandable that in writing about, for example, Oscar Wilde, Hitchens would discuss Wilde's avowed political views ("Oscar Wilde's Socialism"), or his infamous morals trial and its cultural and social legacy ("The Wilde Side," "Lord Trouble"), but in none of these essays—the first three in the book—can it be said that Hitchens shows how Wilde the artist "committed political writing," involuntary or otherwise. He begins to examine the supposedly socialist subtext of *The Importance of Being Earnest*, but really about as far as he gets is to assert that through "satirical means" the play subjects "the bourgeoisie order to a merciless critique." Quite obviously something like this could be said about any number of satirical plays or novels, and Hitchens does not at all attempt an analysis of what makes *Earnest* distinctive in its humor beyond the usual emphasis on Wildean one-liners, nor even, finally does he do much to establish that it is a particularly funny or effective play beyond the fact that it does critique the bourgeoisie order. It is rather difficult to regard *The Importance of Being Earnest* as great "political writing" without first of all being able to judge it as simply great theater, of a sort only a writer like Oscar Wilde could have created.

If Hitchens takes up Wilde the playwright only to focus instead on the playwright's political convictions, in *Unacknowledged Legislation*'s two essays on Gore Vidal he really doesn't bother to examine Vidal's fiction much at all (except to summarize the plots of a few of them), instead proceeding quite forthrightly to discuss such things as Vidal's failed political career, his defense of sexual freedom, his views on politics and political history more generally. He does nicely sum up the issues with which Vidal is most often concerned, but one does wonder how much Hitchens is willing to indulge Vidal his anti-imperialist views, for example, now that Hitchens himself has apparently come to see some virtue in American imperialist actions in response to Arab and Islamist extremism. More significantly, Hitchens's choice to extol Vidal the political "thinker" in this essay only highlights the absence of real critical scrutiny of Vidal's fiction (or even the essays, for that matter), which, in my view, does very little service to Vidal's ultimate reputation as a writer. If you believe, as I do, that the literary merit of Vidal's work is seriously in question, reading Hitchens on Vidal is going to do very little to alter your judgment.

The same thing is true of Hitchens's considerations of Kipling, of Wodehouse, and of Christopher Isherwood. One does not read Hitchens for insight into the hidden virtues of underestimated writers (a fact that becomes even clearer in his Orwell book). One learns that Hitchens himself has a lingering affection for these writers, but not much that would convince the uninitiated to read them voluntarily. There are some essays in *Unacknowledged Legislation* that dwell more closely on the identifiably literary accomplishments of certain writers, but even they usually make their way back to the social and political context within which Hitchens apparently feels comfortable confining his interest in works of literature. His essay on Anthony Powell, for example, admirably describes various volumes of *Dance to the Music of Time*, but even when pointing out the virtues of this series of novels, Hitchens is led finally to conclude that "the chief attainment" of Powell's maturation as a novelist was his "evolution from a moral, even prim, spectator to fully engaged social and political raconteur." His reasonably insightful essay on Philip Larkin is ultimately interested in delineating "the British condition," which can be identified as "that of Larkin without the poetry." "The Road to West Egg," on *The Great Gatsby* (one of the few selections in the book to venture into American literature), struggles to establish that the novel's themes are "timeless," but really this essay only rehearses the usual platitudes about the way in which Gatsby "captures the evaporating memory of the American Eden while connecting it to the advent of the New World of smartness and thuggery and corruption" and thus firmly attaches it to its particular time and place.

No one who reads the essays collected in *Unacknowledged Legislation* could deny Hitchens's intelligence, his grasp of political history, his general familiarity with the writers about whom he writes, or his sincerity when claiming a love of literature. But as a literary critic he is clearly more inspired by the examples set by the writers he surveys, by their personal integrity or consistency of attitude than by the enduring literary qualities of what they've written. This biographical approach is perhaps most prominently on display in *Why Orwell Matters*. Hitchens's most sustained work of ostensible literary criticism (or at least most extended examination of a single literary figure), this book also thus reveals what he appears to value most in the career of a writer like Orwell, who entered the "public sphere" in a very explicit way, committing political writing quite voluntarily indeed. Hitchens admires above all Orwell's integrity, his moral courage, the consistency and prescience of his political views. In short, Hitchens presents Orwell as a kind of symbol of the writer/intellectual as truth-teller and public conscience, a role Christopher Hitchens himself has certainly seemed willing to assume in his own career as what we now call a public intellectual.

In *Why Orwell Matters* Hitchens doesn't argue that Orwell matters because of the intrinsic merits of anything he wrote in particular, but instead seeks to show how Orwell avoided the excesses of both the left and the right, how he maintained a principled opposition to imperialism, why his blindness to feminism and to the future importance of the United States should not be held against him, why his anti-communism was far from reactionary. For Christopher Hitchens, George Orwell was a great man. Although I have my doubts that Orwell was quite the moral exemplar Hitchens makes him out to be, I am willing to concede he had plenty of admirable qualities. And by no means would I claim that Orwell wrote nothing that will survive purely on its literary excellence—many of the essays especially remain persuasive and provocative, and *1984* will probably also retain its power to disturb. But that Orwell was in some ways a superior human being does not establish that he was an equally superior writer whose work will stand the test of time as literary compositions separate from the political context that gave them their initial appeal.

In the one short chapter in *Why Orwell Matters* devoted specifically to Orwell's fiction, about the best Hitchens can do in defense of the pre-Animal Farm novels is to claim them "as the forerunners to the . . . 'Angry Young Man' literary productions of the 1950s, and also to the existentialist and absurdist works of that period, as well as to the gritty 'Northern' school of social realism which found its way into early British cinema as well as onto the London stage." (He doesn't go so far as to suggest that this early fiction is itself as accomplished as the later "literary productions" identified.) But ultimately he concedes that "[t]hese four pre-war efforts constitute a sort of amateur throat-clearing." While one can appreciate the honesty of this conclusion (even its soundness as a literary judgment), consigning Orwell's fiction, the work for which he had the highest hopes, to such a brief discussion at the back of the book hardly advances the case for Orwell's preeminence. Only a few additional paragraphs in the same chapter are devoted to analysis of *Animal Farm* and *1984*, and even here Hitchens is most at pains to establish Orwell's place in the battle against totalitarianism and to emphasize what Orwell had learned from "decades of polemical battles."

In the book's concluding chapter, Hitchens more or less confesses that his interest in Orwell is not really literary: "The disputes and debates and combats in which George Orwell took part are receding into history, but the manner in which he conducted himself as a writer and participant has a reasonable chance of remaining as a historical example of its own." In the end Hitchens has probably measured Orwell's legacy correctly. He is more likely to survive because of what he stood for rather than what he wrote, as a figure from intellectual history rather than literary history. But Hitchens's esteem for Orwell's example nevertheless illuminates the premises upon which he usually proceeds as a literary critic. The poets and novelists Hitchens writes about are important to him for what they represent, for the way in which they illustrate historical movements and political ideas, for their beliefs and their habits of mind. Presumably, from Hitchens's perspective about the most praiseworthy thing that might be said about an author is that he "conducted himself" as a writer particularly well, not that he (or she—although Hitchens considers very few if any women writers in any of his reviews and essays) actually wrote something especially admirable.

Morris Dickstein and Historical Criticism

Readers of Morris Dickstein's *Dancing in the Dark: A Cultural History of the Great Depression* (2009) should find it an agreeable survey of the cultural expressions of the 1930s that reveals how the Depression years were portrayed and understood by those living through them. Readers of Dickstein's previous books will recognize its method, a fastidious interrogation of novels, films, and other works of art for their historical resonances and mutual assumptions, their ability to show how an entire culture at a particular time is "thinking." Readers less interested in Dickstein's signature critical approach or in the context his earlier books provide nevertheless could easily enough from *Dancing in the Dark* be made aware of "Depression culture" in a coherent and often insightful way. Dickstein's painstaking scrutiny of texts for their clues to cultural developments can occasionally get bogged down in some turgid writing, but that he can be an acute analyst of these texts within the framework of a consistently applied historical criticism is undeniable.

While I don't find this sort of historical criticism invalid—there is ultimately nothing wrong with situating a work of art or literature in its period and cultural milieu, as long as the limits of this strategy as a way to "understand" the work are acknowledged—I often find Dickstein's relentless pursuit of the strategy tedious and of questionable service to literature. Since a great deal of his criticism has been focused on post-World War II American fiction, I think that Dickstein has especially done some disservice to contemporary fiction, my own critical bailiwick, distorting its achievement and finally reducing it to a function as barometer of the cultural and political changes that have taken place in the United States between 1945 and the present.

I make this criticism regretfully, as Dickstein's 1979 book, *Gates of Eden*, was probably more responsible for setting me on a path of study of contemporary fiction than any other critical book I read or any course I took. It introduced me to the work of experimental writers such as John Barth and Donald Barthelme, of whom I don't think I'd ever heard at the time, and although I could sense even when reading the book as an undiscriminating undergraduate that Dickstein didn't entirely approve of their fiction, especially the Barthelme of the late '60s and after, just the suggestion that Barthelme was "radical" (Dickstein meant to associate him with the decadent, Weatherman phase of 60s radicalism) was enough to make me want to read his books posthaste.

Actually, much of Dickstein's analysis of the fiction of the 1960s still holds up, as I discovered when I recently re-read the book, even if the tacit impatience with postmodernism seems more apparent to me now. (The term "postmodernism" is never used, however; Dickstein in 1979 preferred to identify writers like Barth and Barthelme as modernists, emphasizing the continuity between the formal experimentation of modernism and that which came to be called postmodernism. Dickstein thinks that late modernism radicalized itself beyond redemption in the work of writers such as Rudolph Wurlitzer, but while I can't agree that the experimental impulse inevitably leads to an aesthetic impasse, his implicit suggestion that the adventurous writing of the 1960s and 1970s was really a second flowering of modernism usefully emphasizes that "postmodernism" was first of all a phenomenon of literary history, not a reorientation of history itself.) Above all, his recognition that the fiction of the 1960s represents a significant achievement still seems audacious:

> In a topsy-turvy age that often turned trash into art and art into trash, that gaily pursued topical fascination and ephemeral performances and showed a real genius for self-consuming artifacts—an age that sometimes valued art too little because it loved raw life too much—novels were written that are among the handful of art-works, few enough in any age, that are likely to endure. It's a bizarre prospect, but the sixties are as likely to be remembered through novels as through anything else they left behind.

Dickstein finds much that is praiseworthy in the fiction of Thomas Pynchon, Joseph Heller, Kurt Vonnegut, and even Barth and Barthelme, despite his judgment that they ultimately take things too far. However ambivalent his reaction to the most adventurous of adventurous fiction, and however much attention he gives to writers whose work will not, in my opinion, "endure," such as Bellow and Mailer, Dickstein's consideration of the experimental fiction of the sixties inspired me at least to take this fiction seriously and to discover for myself whether it produced work "likely to endure."

Unfortunately, the very passage I have quoted, I now see, also signals the real limitations of Dickstein's approach, of the assumptions about fiction's utility as a clue to culture. The last sentence arguably implies that the novels of the era will last because they are the best way to "remember" the sixties. For those who lived through the era, they will continue to evoke it; for those future readers who did not, they will still enable a cultural "remembering" that will likely allow us to get a glimpse of the kind of "topical" and "ephemeral" attractions Dickstein describes in the rest of the passage. These novels will be "left behind" for scholars and others interested in that "topsy-turvy age" to recreate it, either critically or imaginatively. Fiction is ultimately of value, especially fiction particularly attuned to the social wavelength of its period, as a window onto history. It perhaps enlivens history in a way that straight historical narrative or cultural criticism cannot, but otherwise it remains an adjunct to the study of culture in its historical manifestations.

My own initial response to *Gates of Eden* demonstrates that it is possible to read the book as an illuminating appraisal of American fiction of the 1950s and 1960s, but turning to Dickstein's other writing on postwar fiction only confirms that ultimately his purpose seems to be to pin postwar writers down as specimens of their time and place, at best figures in a procession of "tendencies." In the essays "The Face in the Mirror: The Eclipse of Distance in Contemporary Fiction" and "Ordinary People: Carver, Ford and Blue-Collar Realism" (both reprinted in *A Mirror in the Roadway*, Dickstein's explicit defense of realism), he extends his survey of postwar fiction into the 1970s and 1980s. In the first, he notes a shift in the 1970s toward novels "built around characters who are the very self and voice of the author," exemplified by Philip Roth, William Styron, and John Irving. In the second he discusses the rise of minimalism in the work of Raymond Carver, as well as the subsequent move away from minimalism to "a more expansive, more full-bodied fiction" in the work of Richard Ford and Russell Banks. In the latter he predicts a further shift to "some transformed and heightened version of the social novel." Clearly Dickstein is most interested in contemporary fiction as an opportunity to chart developments in fiction's way of registering social realities. Chronicling the rise and fall of trends in fiction is not necessarily a trivial activity, but in Dickstein's case the single-minded manner in which he pursues the task does threaten to make criticism an intellectual version of fashion journalism.

Leopards in the Temple (2002) is probably Dickstein's summary statement of the historical progression of postwar American fiction. Subtitled "The Transformation of American Fiction 1945-1970," it again focuses on the 1950s and 1960s, this time treating only fiction but otherwise covering much of the same ground scrutinized in *Gates of Eden*. The biggest change in approach to the fiction of this period is a considerable narrowing of the terrain on which Dickstein is willing to cast his critical eye, leaving experimental or postmodern fiction out of view almost completely. He instead devotes most of the book to discussions of well-publicized mainstream writers such as Gore Vidal, Truman Capote, Mailer, James Jones, Jack Kerouac, James Baldwin, John Updike, Bellow, and Roth, although there are a few welcome considerations of Paul Bowles, Nabokov, Heller, and Vonnegut. Dickstein's implicit dismissal of experimental fiction is perhaps best exemplified in his discussion of John Barth's *End of the Road*, which Dickstein calls "Barth's best novel" and is included in *Leopards in the Temple* in the first place mainly because it illustrates the "road" theme Dickstein traces from Kerouac to other writers of the '50s and early '60s. His attitude toward Barth's later metafiction, truly his most important achievement, well beyond *End of the Road*, is surely encapsulated in his observation that "In *Lost in the Funhouse* and *Chimera* Barth's genial narrators soon grow as heartily sick of [their] self-consciousness as we do."

One can legitimately find the work of John Barth and other metafictionists not to one's liking without distorting the fact of its prominence during the period Dickstein is examining. It is hardly credible to suggest that the 1960s are most appropriately represented by Bellow, Malamud, and James Baldwin, which Dickstein does in his final chapter by highlighting their work rather than the postmodern writers, whose work rebelled against the quiescent realism preferred by the gatekeepers of literary culture, much as others rebelled against the constraints of conformity and established practice in other arts, in politics, and in culture more generally during this time. A survey of the "transformation" of American fiction after World War II that willfully excludes this work is finally hard to take seriously.

Leopards in the Temple posits a postwar literary history that begins with war novelists, proceeds through the early fiction of certain writers who first came to public attention immediately after the war, such as Vidal and Capote, further through sensation-causing writers such as Kerouac and J.D Salinger, and, with some pauses along the way to acknowledge a few other noteworthy authors, winds up affirming the centrality of culturally sanctioned novelists such as Bellow, Baldwin, and Mailer. Another history of postwar fiction is possible, however, one that begins with, say, John Hawkes, emphasizes Nabokov's work beyond *Lolita*, carefully considers William Gaddis, includes James Purdy and Thomas Berger along with Joseph Heller, and takes as the apogee of the period the work of Pynchon, Barth, Robert Coover, and Donald Barthelme. Dickstein's history is a history of American culture as reflected in his chosen authors and books; the alternative history is more properly a literary history of the years 1945-60, one that focuses on the response of writers to the legacy and the challenges of modernism by extending that legacy through fiction that continued to challenge readers' expectations and that, in my opinion, more accurately encompasses the writers whose work will still likely be read once this period more firmly recedes into literal history.

What now alienates me the most from Dickstein's critical method, however, are the grand generalizations he makes about the practice of fiction, generalizations that interpose great distance between the critic and the texts he/she ostensibly tries to illuminate. He writes, for example, that for novelists of the 1940s and 1950s

> They were obsessed more with Oedipal struggle than with class struggle, concerned about the limits of civilization rather than the conflicts within civilization. Their premises were more Freudian than Marxist. Auschwitz and Hiroshima had set them thinking about the nature and destiny of man, and relative affluence gave them the leisure to focus on spiritual confusions in their own lives.

How does Dickstein know what "they" were thinking? How can "they," as opposed to individual writers, be thinking anything except insofar as the critic has self-selected a few of "them," invested them with "premises" and speculated about "their" social standing ("relative affluence") and the state of their souls ("spiritual confusions")? Occasionally Dickstein does offer an interesting critical reading of a particular text, as when he observes of *Catcher in the Rye* that "Holden's adventures in New York are really a series of Jewish jokes, at once sad, funny, and self-accusing," but the overwhelmingly dominant impression left by *Leopards in the Temple*, and by Morris Dickstein's books as a whole, is that fiction is most worthwhile as a leading indicator not just of just of writers', but an entire culture's temporal obsessions. If I thought this was the foremost reason to read novels, I'd probably never read another one.

~

Hershel Parker: Criticism vs. Scholarship

*I*t is finally unclear exactly what audience Hershel Parker had in mind in writing *Melville Biography: An Inside Narrative*. Parker is a distinguished academic scholar, but while a great deal of the book is preoccupied with laying out Parker's side of an academic quarrel, the tone of his exposition of the controversy doesn't suggest he expects the other side to respond—certainly not as part of an ongoing scholarly debate. On the other hand, the nature of this dispute is sufficiently arcane that it probably would not really be of interest to general readers, although Parker's animus against his various detractors is expressed trenchantly (and often) enough that these readers might find his demonstrations of malfeasance occasionally entertaining.

Presumably, admirers of Herman Melville would be potential readers of *Melville Biography*, but unfortunately most of the discussion in the book requires some prior familiarity not just with Melville's life and work but specifically with Hershel Parker's own previous writing about Melville, most obviously his two-volume biography, published in 1996 and 2002, respectively. At best this book serves as a supplement of sorts to the biography, as we learn about the assumptions behind Parker's practice as a biographer, and the final section of the book, "The Biographer in the Workshop," focuses on material not included in the biography and does provide interesting information about such things as the influence of copyright law on Melville's short-lived career as novelist and his relationship with Nathaniel Hawthorne. Still, it would seem that readers who might be interested in such information about Herman Melville would have gone to the biography first before taking up this postscript.

Melville Biography is most interesting as a continuation of a quarrel Parker has been conducting for years—arguably throughout his whole career as a scholar—with academic criticism. The terms of this quarrel roughly correspond to the opposition between "criticism" and "scholarship," with Parker's own work exemplifying the latter and what Parker perceives to be the academic establishment predominantly practicing the former. As the title of this new book suggests, Parker's scholarly work has mostly been biographical (as well as mostly focused on Herman Melville), culminating in the two-volume biography but even before that concentrating on biographical and historical context as the indispensable foundation of serious literary study. Since the death of Jay Leyda, creator of *The Melville Log*, literally the day-by-day documentation of Melville's life, Parker has taken over as the proprietor/editor of the Log (and to his credit has expanded it substantially), just one indication of the way he has devoted his academic career to retrieving as much concrete information about Herman Melville as possible.

Parker is not interested in accumulating this information just to know more about Melville the historical figure or human personality. He believes that literary criticism cannot proceed at all unless it arises first from reliable knowledge of the writer's circumstances, especially the circumstances related to the work's composition and publication. Parker has frequently expressed his disdain for criticism and interpretation that ignores possible problems with the status of the text itself and blithely comes to conclusions based on corrupted or uncertain texts. His most thorough examination of this issue is his 1984 book, *Flawed Texts and Verbal Icons*, in which he discusses such textual problems not just in Melville but also Henry James, Stephen Crane, Mark Twain, and, bringing the subject farther into the present, Norman Mailer. "It seems that treating the author as an abstracted, olympian power," Parker writes at the end of the first chapter, "frees critics to celebrate nonsensical texts and adventitious meanings in texts where the words, but not all the meanings, are the author's; and treating the text the author created as if it were merely a hypothetical concept, frees them to identify 'the text itself' as the published text or the revised and republished text."

Parker's point is that too much academic criticism, in the form of "close reading," which focuses its attention solely on "the text," carelessly assumes the reliability and authenticity of the text being read. Before venturing an interpretation or asserting the historical or cultural forces the work allegedly makes visible, Parker asks, shouldn't we have some confidence that the text we're citing is the text the author wanted us to read? Even if, as in the case of Crane, the author acquiesced to revisions in order to get the work published, should we accept a palpably inferior text because the author didn't or wasn't able to signal a preference for another version (in Crane's case because of his early death)? Aren't the conclusions a critic might reach about a literary work questionable if the text of that work is itself questionable?

These are entirely relevant questions, ones that academic critics should take seriously, that raise issues transcending the debate about the role of the scholar vs. the role of the critic. Surely the critic venturing to claim an authoritative interpretation or close reading of a particular work should have some sense of the text's own authority. Although the most radical implication of Parker's detailed explication of the messy textual histories of these books by Crane, Twain, and Melville is that there might be some works for which a final, definitive text isn't possible, even that finally no such text is really possible for any work of literature, literary criticism that simply ignores the problems Parker identifies is either willfully negligent or shows little respect not just for those scholars who work at providing conscientiously edited texts but also for the process of literary creation, the essential messiness of which is reflected in the realities of publication, even when the latter don't actively mutilate the writer's intended text.

Parker weakens his case, however, by his inclination to blur all distinctions and label anyone who favors interpretation or close analysis a "New Critic." This is made evident directly in the title of *Flawed Texts and Verbal Icons* in its explicit evocation of the "verbal icon," W.K. Wimsatt's notion of the literary text as an aesthetic object made of words, to be approached and appreciated as such by the critic conscious of the work's aesthetic integrity. Parker believes that the original New Critics' dogmatic rejection of "extrinsic evidence," evidence not directly to be found in the verbal disposition of the text at hand, was so influential that their "avoidance of 'textual bibliography' in all its aspects, including study of compositional evidence, has prevailed during all later fashions in criticism." Indeed, "even the deconstructionists in practice treated any text as a New Critical given, however thoroughly they would then proceed to deconstruct it," and the New Historicists, who would seem to have retrieved "extrinsic evidence" from opprobrium, unfortunately "proceeded to write history and literary history as if research had all been done before, once and for all, prior to, say around 1940" (*Melville Biography*). These postmodern historicists "were no such fools as to hope to tell the truth: there was no such thing as truth."

Parker is dedicated to the idea that there is truth to be applied to works of literature, and finally the influence of New Criticism has been to emphasize coherence of interpretation over truth, the integrity of close reading over scholarship that uncovers the truth. But while there is some plausibility to the notion that deconstruction (at least as practiced by Derrida) has affinities with New Critical close reading, to the extent that New Criticism was an attempt to place the study of literature at the center of the English curriculum, in effect to place literature itself at the center of this curriculum, deconstruction was less interested in close reading as a strategy for appreciating literature as a means for raising questions about the nature of human communication, ultimately about the nature of human thought. Although Derrida's reading strategies could certainly be used to examine a literary text in a way that would be compatible with New Criticism—emphasizing uncertainty, ambiguity, "gaps," etc,—the rise of deconstruction (of what is called "critical theory" more generally) most immediately signaled a move away from "appreciation" of literature to its more detached "interrogation." Both critical theory and new historicism, however much they avoided "textual bibliography," also unfortunately tended to avoid literature as well. In their shared goals of enhancing appreciation of literature as the actual subject of the discipline of literary study, Hershel Parker the scholar surely has much more in common with New Critics than with critical theorists, new historicists, and academic critics engaged in cultural studies, all of whom have done much more than the New Critics ever did to make Parker's kind of textual and biographical scholarship passé.

Even if you accept that there is a divide between "criticism" and "scholarship" of the kind Parker laments, and even if you accept that New Criticism may have helped to orient literary study away from biographical criticism, text editing, and historical investigation (all of which nevertheless remained visible scholarly approaches even during the heyday of New Criticism), it is a not a necessary conclusion that New Critical formalism was inherently hostile to traditional scholarship. For one thing, conscientious proponents of close reading would be foolish to dismiss attempts to establish reliable texts or to get historical information right for the very reason that Parker's own discussions in *Flawed Texts and Verbal Icons* provides: A reading of a flawed text is ultimately a flawed reading. For an approach that implicitly holds every word in a literary text to be potentially significant, perhaps crucial, to disdain a concern that all the words be justifiably in place would undermine the whole project. Moreover, New Criticism's skepticism about non-textual "evidence" came from a resistance to "readings" that, in drawing on history, biography, or politics, diverted attention from the experience of reading the work to these other subjects, not from a lack of respect for the accomplishments of literary scholarship.

In *Melville Biography: An Inside Narrative*, Parker's ire is primarily directed at such current academic critics as Andrew Delbanco and Richard Brodhead (currently President of Duke University), both of whom could be called "New Critics" only in the expanded, indeterminate definition Parker has given it in order to identify the source of these critics' disparagement of his work, especially the biography of Melville. I myself find Parker's defense of his biography against the criticisms made by Delbanco and Brodhead persuasive, but also don't understand why these criticisms can't simply be addressed in their own terms rather than generalizing them into a perpetual struggle between what in Parker's analysis are ancient enemies. Not only is this likely to seem to most potential readers of the book a rather musty characterization of the issues, belonging to an era now long superseded by one in which both criticism and scholarship have been radically transformed, but the terms of the debate seem to have become so personal for Hershel Parker that his book can at times be uncomfortable to read as well. It is clear enough that Parker feels his biography was unfairly treated (and indeed perhaps it was), but a grievance sustained over the length of a 500-page book can finally wear a little thin.

Flawed Texts and Verbal Icons is an illuminating and important book, well worth reading even by those who might consider Parker's scholarly approach hopelessly old-fashioned, who might instead come to recognize that inaccurate or corrupted texts are just as threatening to "extrinsic" historical and cultural generalizations using literary works as critical specimens as to "intrinsic" explication. As long as literary texts remain the ostensible focus of literary study (which of course is even now not always the case), their reliability will always be a relevant issue—not to mention its relevance simply to readers who want to feel confident the books they are reading adequately represent what their authors intended them to read. *Melville Biography*, unfortunately, is of much less interest, although perhaps it could persuade a few to give Parker's biography a try, or to pursue the underlying points of contention more directly through *Flawed Texts and Verbal Icons* instead.

≈

Postmodern Fiction and Academic Criticism

*J*oseph M. Conte's *Design and Debris: A Chaotics of Postmodern American Fiction* is one of the numerous studies of American postmodernism that attempt to account for the postmodern in fiction by focusing on a particular formal quality or philosophical orientation that further specifies what makes a "postmodern" text distinctive beyond the vaguely radical connotation generally associated with the term. In this book Conte proposes a dual impulse in certain postmodern texts, toward on the one hand the disintegration of presumed order, both in the world and as the world is represented in fiction, and on the other toward the cultivation of an emergent order out of the disorder these texts faithfully render. "Design" is thus as much a defining feature of postmodern fiction as the "debris" of contemporary life this fiction must also acknowledge.

Postmodernism has proven to be among the most examined phenomena in postwar American fiction. Not only were postmodern authors and practices ("postmodern" as we now retrospectively apply the term, at least) more or less at the center of scholarly interest in contemporary fiction for the first decade or so after its acceptance as an academic field of study, but even now, more than four decades after its emergence as literature's contribution to the "radical" cultural movements of the 1960s, postmodernism continues to engage the interest of academic critics. While some such critics are more interested in postmodernism as a cultural orientation than as an approach to the writing of fiction, Conte belongs among those who have attempted to delineate the radicalism of postmodern fiction in its departure from conventional modes of representation and its concomitant intensification of modernist formal experiment by examining the radical literary strategies at work in postmodern texts.

Conte focuses both on what must now be called canonical postmodernist novels such as De Lillo's *White Noise*, Coover's *The Universal Baseball Association*, and Pynchon's *Gravity's Rainbow*, as well as less-discussed works such as John Hawkes's *Travesty*, Kathy Acker's *Empire of the Senseless*, and Gilbert Sorrentino's *Pack of Lies*. *Travesty* is Conte's first and most compelling example in fleshing out his claim ("design and debris," in fact, is a phrase taken from this novel), and it is one of his book's chief virtues that it brings this welcome attention to Hawkes, whose work may represent, in such books as *The Beetle Leg*, *The Goose on the Grave*, and *The Lime Twig*, the earliest appearance of what would later be characterized as postmodernism and whose body of work as a whole stands as one of the greatest achievements in postwar American fiction. He has become an unduly neglected figure in the consideration of literary postmodernism, and Conte's discussion of *Travesty* demonstrates Hawkes's centrality to the practice.

According to Conte, "As a postmodern novelist, Hawkes does not shrink before the proposition of 'unmaking' or decreative force; he extols the complementarity of the two terms; and finally, he proposes the existence of an orderly disorder." *Travesty* "illustrates the tenuousness of authoritarian control as it slips into madness, the fragility of pattern as it dissolves into irregularity; and it proposes the revelation of some hidden order in the scatter of random occurrences, some more profound design within the welter of chaos." This seems an accurate description of the thematic burden of *Travesty*, although the extent to which the "design and debris" strategy informs the novel's own formal design is not really explored very fully. One could argue that Hawkes's dictum that he began to write fiction "on the assumption that the true enemies of the novel were plot, character, setting, and theme" committed him to a design and debris aesthetic by which Hawkes reconstituted fiction from the shards of convention through what he called "totality of vision or structure." Unfortunately, Conte confines his discussion of design and debris to the thematic exposition of its salience as revealed in the "design" of its main character, who is driving a car hurtling at high speed toward an inevitable crash, and who discusses his intentions with his captive passengers. From Conte's analysis, one might conclude that *Travesty*'s narrative manifests "design and debris" allegorically, but not that Hawkes has fundamentally altered the formal assumptions of fiction in a way that is distinctively "postmodern."

If critical examination of postmodern fiction has in general exhibited a bias that distorts our perception of postmodern, experimental fiction and prevents full appreciation of its expressed qualities, it would be a bias toward the thematic, broadly philosophical implications that can be drawn from it. Most academic critics of postmodern fiction celebrate its antifoundational or "subversive" qualities, its capacity to incorporate cutting-edge critical theories and new ideas in science or epistemology, but rarely do they attend predominantly to the purely aesthetic consequences of postmodernism's various dismantlings of narrative convention. While the debris of inherited form lies in the wake of postmodern strategies, "design" is also an ultimate product of those strategies. Form is not discarded—putting aside the question of whether any work of fiction could be truly formless—but instead made more elastic, often through highlighting "form" as a specific issue of concern within the text itself. The real legacy of American postmodern fiction will be a demonstrable expansion of the range of possible formal variations of which fiction is capable, beyond even the initial expansion of those possibilities achieved by the modernists, and more analyses of how a writer such as John Hawkes contributed to this legacy are needed.

The fiction of Kathy Acker also seems especially illustrative of a postmodern strategy of design and debris, and Conte does examine *Empire of the Senseless* in the context of its radical formal iconoclasm. As Conte notes, "Acker can be expected to disregard the traditional rules of fiction." Her work employs discontinuity, collage and parody in a way that makes it an exemplar of Hawkes's dismissal of "the true enemies of fiction" almost as provocative as Hawkes's own; in some instances it is even more thoroughgoing in its rejection of narrative coherence. Unfortunately, Conte chooses to put most of his emphasis on the way Acker's iconoclasm serves an ulterior political purpose, insisting that "the scumbling of levels of discourse in the novel reflects Acker's anarchistic methodology, undermining the reader's presuppositions of dominant-intellectual and subordinate-proletarian cultural positions." It is hard to deny that Kathy Acker included among her ambitions the desire to upend the "patriarchal order," but to whatever extent her fiction attracts future readers it will be because of its "anarchistic" formal energies, not its analysis of "cultural positions."

That Acker may have been motivated to create her unconventional texts at least in part by the belief they might implicitly undermine class and gender constructions does not ultimately determine how their formal/aesthetic effects will be perceived. As in his discussion of Hawkes, Conte is ultimately more interested in Acker's thematic treatment of "design and debris," concluding that "Acker finds that even in the domain of anarchy—in nomadic space, after the disruption of the state apparatus, where women ride motorcycles—there must be discipline present." But the real "discipline" Acker brings to her fiction is in the alternate "order" she provides despite the apparent anarchy of her means. Only if, in fact, readers catch on to the design of a work like *Em-*

pire of the Senseless—unorthodox but nevertheless present—will such a work continue to find its readers. Conte identifies this design as rising from a conceptualism by which "methodology is directly supportive of the concept" animating it, but it is the way in which the reader can discern the relationship between methodology and concept that ultimately gives Acker's fiction its literary interest. Acker's particular application of conceptualism to fiction is what future readers are likely to find compelling about it, while the concept itself will likely come to seem rather reduced in its power to provoke.

Conte does a much more adequate job of accounting for the formally challenging postmodernism of Gilbert Sorrentino, Harry Mathews, and John Barth, writers Conte identifies as "proceduralists" who "invent forms without knowing the precise manner of text that will be generated." Such works embody design and debris by revealing "an immanent design within their apparently chaotic distribution of materials." The designation "proceduralist" seems most immediately and most accurately applicable to Mathews's fiction, since his association with the Oulipo is well-known and since the Oulipian credo specifically calls for the use of rules and formal constraints in creating literary texts. "Procedural" seems less obviously descriptive of the fiction of Barth and Sorrentino, and Conte usefully examines the way Barth uses "arabesque" in his novel *The Last Voyage of Somebody the Sailor* (and implicitly in other of his books) to create "nested frames" which provide a "recursive symmetry" organizing the narrative, as well as the way Sorrentino in his *Pack of Lies* trilogy employs a complex patterning of constraints, some perhaps fully apparent only to Sorrentino, to give the novels a unity that is not conventionally serial. Conte's concluding remarks about Sorrentino aptly capture an essential element of this writer's work:

> Sorrentino's conviction that structure can generate content in his fiction relies upon the reciprocal influence between author and text. The author invents the structure of the work, but that structure compels his performance in ways that he had not anticipated.

POSTMODERN FICTION AND ACADEMIC CRITICISM

If Conte's discussions of Barth and Sorrentino illuminate qualities of their work that have not previously been as clearly identified, his chapters on *White Noise*, *The Universal Baseball Association* and *Gravity's Rainbow* to some extent retrod old ground in the critical consideration of these novels. Conte uses information theory, systems theory, complexity theory, and the ideas of the mathematician Benoir Mandelbrot to map the design and debris strategy at work in these iconic postmodern texts, and while the readings that result seem perfectly cogent in elucidating that strategy, nothing very fresh is really added to the commentary on the novels themselves beyond what has already been offered in the voluminous existing criticism of them. At best they demonstrate that such works readily lend themselves to a critical approach that is itself "postmodern" in its assumptions and its resources, although in my view their complexity is less a consequence of their concordance with the more abstruse levels of postmodern theory than their capacity to stand up to critical and interpretive scrutiny from a multitude of perspectives and still seem not exhausted in their potential to reveal meaning and provide for a bracing reading experience.

A final chapter attempts to bring the study of postmodern fiction into the digital era, announcing that "The paradigm shift from print to digital culture should be acknowledged as a defining aspect of postmodernism." Containing relatively brief analyses of the work of William Gibson, Richard Powers, and De Lillo's *Underworld* as examples of fiction that "though bound to the present order... is provocatively enhanced by an engagement with the terms and conditions of the information age," it essentially reaffirms the accomplishments of the "print order," at least in the form of postmodern fiction, which "offers certain palliatives for...symptoms of technological neurasthenia." For Conte

> Finally, postmodern fiction offers relief for the "pixelated," those viewers stunned into anomie by the bombardment of pixels—the smallest image-forming units of the video display. It turns out that print on paper still has the capacity to evoke images and ideas as compelling as any we might encounter in the flicker of a screen.

It seems to me that here Conte has stretched the "postmodern" to the limits of its utility as a critical concept. If the "paradigm shift" ushering in digital culture is a "defining aspect of postmodernism," why should it not require the postmodern critic's unhesitating embrace? If Conte is right that what he calls "electronic composition" has not yet produced its "masterly" author, then doesn't this shift mark a break, a period of transition between postmodernism and a new dispensation that will embrace the dominance of the digital? Surely "postmodern" cannot continue to be the designation of choice for describing all literary or philosophical projects that show the world to be more complex, beliefs about it more necessarily relative, than we once imagined. Nor can it indefinitely remain essentially a synonym for "unconventional" or "experimental." Unconventional writers might be motivated simply by the desire to try out alternative strategies, not to seek out those that are already acceptably postmodern as critics and theorists have defined the strategy.

It may be that academic criticism will turn to electronic forms as the subject of "advanced" analysis. This would certainly be more in keeping with the direction academic criticism has taken in the last twenty-five years: away from the consideration of works of literature as a self-sufficient task and toward approaches that enhance the role of academic criticism itself. In the study of contemporary fiction this would mean less emphasis on identifying and examining the most significant writers and works and more on the cultural and cognitive implications of the electronic medium itself. Literary study, or at least that branch of it devoted to the contemporary, could merge with media study. If present and future writers are to be provided with the same sort of critical attention that has been accorded to the postmodernists, it will probably be necessary that literary criticism be rejuvenated in a form free of institutional requirements. It will require critics once again interested first of all in literature and not in the status of their own critical projects or the interrogation of trends in culture as a whole.

3
CRITICAL SUCCESSES

PART 3

CRITICAL SUCCESSES

None of the critics discussed in this final section succeed in the same way, nor do they necessarily succeed because they affirm my own critical principles. They in fact greatly differ among themselves in their focus and assumptions. They are united, however, in their commitment to the autonomous value of art and literature, and to the notion that the experience of art and literature has a kind of autonomy of its own, to which the critic must first of all turn in order to account for its effects. A common source of attention for many of these critics is the effect of style, which, since literature is a verbal art, appropriately seems the element literary critics would find the most crucial influence on the reading experience.

Several of the critics included here are of course prominent figures in postwar literary criticism (Susan Sontag, Harold Bloom, for example), but their ideas and their legacy still seem to me quite relevant to present practice. The final three essays examine books notably representing present practice. One, Michael Gorra's *Portrait of a Novel*, illustrates how the divide between academic and general interest criticism might be closed, while the other two are written by critics who show us, through the vitality of their criticism, how this divide needlessly separates resourceful and intelligent critics from a potentially receptive audience. Both of them point the way forward for literary criticism in the digital age, partly by using their criticism as an opportunity to reflect—and provoke reflection—on its own ultimate purposes.

Susan Sontag

In his review of Susan Sontag's journals, Daniel Mendelsohn contends that Sontag, in her practice at least, was not really "against interpretation" at all:

> The essays in *Against Interpretation* and in *Styles of Radical Will* may champion, famously, the need not for "a hermeneutics but an erotics of Art," but what is so striking is that there is not anything very erotic about these essays; they are, in fact, all hermeneutics. In the criticism, as in the journals, the eros is all from the neck up.

A little later he asserts that

> this astoundingly gifted interpreter, so naturally skilled at peeling away trivial-seeming exteriors to reveal deeper cultural meanings—or at teasing out the underlying significance of surface features to which you might not have given much attention ("people run beautifully in Godard movies")—fought mightily to affect an "aesthetic" disdain for content.

Mendelsohn is pretty clearly attempting to turn Sontag's actual strengths as a critic—"peeling away" and "teasing out"—against her in order to question the critical agenda with which Sontag began her career as literary critic, and for which she is still most prominently known. To so baldly label her an "interpreter" is to dismiss her early efforts to rescue the aesthetic pleasures of art from the maw of interpretation and its attempts to "dig 'behind' the text, to find a sub-text which is the true one." She was an interpreter all along and thus the "disdain for content" she expressed could only be an affectation.

Furthermore, Mendelsohn finds that Sontag is untrue to her call for an "erotics of art" because her essays mostly fail to confine themselves to the "sensuous surface" such a call seems to emphasize. Partly this accusation is a necessary gesture in reinforcing Mendelsohn's biographical approach to Sontag's work, through which he maintains that her purported sexual inhibitions fundamentally determined the orientation of her critical responses. "I do not doubt that [Sontag] genuinely wished to experience works of art purely with the senses and the emotions," writes Mendelsohn, "but the author of these celebrated essays is quite plainly the grown-up version of the young girl who, at fifteen, declared her preference for 'virtuosity... technique, organization. . . .'" If there is truth in Mendelsohn's remarks on this subject, however, I don't see why it's necessary to speculate about her sexual hang-ups in order to account for it. In some of her essays Sontag is more of a theoretician than a close reader, but this hardly disqualifies her from holding at the center of her theory about the appropriate response to art a view that such a response ought to be closer to "erotics" than to hermeneutics.

A criticism that lingers over the "sensuous surface" could indeed provide a valuable service, especially if it's a "surface" that might be overlooked in the rush to uncover "content." But it doesn't seem contradictory or inconsistent to go beyond the immediate surface to consider, say, the way various aspects of the surface work together, the way surface sometimes occludes other aesthetically relevant elements, such as the more subtle effects of point of view in fiction or of editing in film. Ultimately, to expect a critic, even one ostensibly dedicated to "sensuous surface," to confine herself to describing those surfaces is to ask her to self-proscribe other critically useful tactics she might employ. Moreover, it is possible to approach a work of art through a move that might be called "interpretation" but that does not amount to interrogating the work for "content." The critic might go beyond obvious surface features to point out less discernible qualities that are relevant to an aesthetic appreciation without thereby working "to translate the elements of the [work] into something else," as Sontag puts it in *Against Interpretation*.

Mendelsohn is suggesting that to be consistent Sontag should have contented herself with the innocent pleasure to be found in the surface features of art, but as Sontag herself reminded us in *Against Interpretation*, "None of us can ever retrieve that innocence before all theory when art knew no need to justify itself, when one did not ask of a work what it said because one knew (or thought one knew) what it did. From now to the end of consciousness, we are stuck with the task of defending art." Sontag wanted to defend art against those who would say that "sensuous surface" is merely a distraction, that the role of the critic is to assure the audience the work is "about" something. For the interpretive critic

> interpretation amounts to the philistine refusal to leave the work of art alone. Real art has the capacity to make us nervous. By reducing the work of art to its content and then interpreting that, one tames the work of art. Interpretation makes art manageable, conformable.

To combat this anti-aesthetic emphasis on "content," Sontag naturally enough sought for a criticism, especially literary criticism, that "brings more attention to form in art":

> If excessive stress on content provokes the arrogance of interpretation, more extended and more thorough descriptions of form would silence. What is needed is a vocabulary—a descriptive, rather than prescriptive, vocabulary—for forms.

This sort of focus on the manifestations of form, more than on the "sensuous" per se, is really what *Against Interpretation* wants to encourage. Sontag wants us to stop looking past the aesthetic thing-in-itself toward the "meaning" it supposedly conceals. This approach to criticism is just a way of making art "manageable," ultimately of making art itself essentially irrelevant. Why go to the trouble of fashioning a "sensuous surface" in the first place if all we're interested in is the latent "content"? Artists just get in the way of our making sense of things.

"Sense" understood as intellectual comprehension. Otherwise, of course, "sense" is precisely what Sontag herself wants to retrieve from the interpreters, although this includes the sensory as part of a unified experience:

Interpretation takes the sensory experience of the work of art for granted, and proceeds from there. This cannot be taken for granted, now. Think of the sheer multiplication of works of art available to every one of us, superadded to the conflicting tastes and odors and sights of the urban environment that bombard our senses. Ours is a culture based on excess, on overproduction; the result is a steady loss of sharpness in our sensory experience. All the conditions of modern life—its material plenitude, its sheer crowdedness—conjoin to dull our sensory faculties. And it is in the light of the condition of our senses, our capacities (rather than those of another age), that the task of the critic must be assessed.

If anything, the conditions making "sharpness in our sensory experience" difficult to attain have only become more pronounced since Sontag wrote this paragraph. Our sensory faculties are surely even duller than they were in the early 1960s, which in retrospect seems a golden age of quiet contemplation.

Sontag's essay "On Style" in *Against Interpretation* contains many passages to warm an aging aesthete's heart:

> Indeed, practically all metaphors for style amount to placing matter on the inside, style on the outside. It would be more to the point to reverse the metaphor. The matter, the subject, is on the outside; the style is on the inside. As Cocteau writes: "Decorative style has never existed. Style is the soul, and unfortunately with us the soul assumes the form of the body." Even if one were to define style as the manner of our appearing, this by no means necessarily entails an opposition between a style that one assumes and one's "true" being. In fact, such a disjunction is extremely rare. In almost every case, our manner of appearing is our manner of being. The mask is the face. . . .
>
> Most critics would agree that a work of art does not "contain" a certain amount of content (or function—as in the case or architecture) embellished by "style." But few address themselves to the positive consequences of what they seem to

have agreed to. What is "content"? Or, more precisely, what is left of the notion of content when we have transcended the antithesis of style (or form) and content? Part of the answer lies in the fact that for a work of art to have "content" is, in itself, a rather special stylistic convention. The great task which remains to critical theory is to examine in detail the formal function of subject-matter. . . .

To treat works of art [as statements] is not wholly irrelevant. But it is, obviously, putting art to use—for such purposes as inquiring into the history of ideas, diagnosing contemporary culture, or creating social solidarity. Such a treatment has little to do with what actually happens when a person possessing some training and aesthetic sensibility looks at a work of art appropriately. A work of art encountered as a work of art is an experience, not a statement or an answer to a question. Art is not only about something; it is something. A work of art is a thing in the world, not just a text or commentary on the world. . . .

Inevitably, critics who regard works of art as statements will be wary of "style," even as they pay lip service to "imagination." All that imagination really means for them, anyway, is the supersensitive rendering of "reality." It is this "reality" snared by the work of art that they continue to focus on, rather than on the extent to which a work of art engages the mind in certain transformations. . . .

In the end, however, attitudes toward style cannot be reformed merely by appealing to the "appropriate" (as opposed to utilitarian) way of looking at works of art. The ambivalence toward style is not rooted in simple error—it would then be quite easy to uproot—but in a passion, the passion of an entire culture. This passion is to protect and defend values traditionally conceived of as lying "outside" art, namely truth and morality, but which remain in perpetual danger of being compromised by art. Behind the ambivalence toward style is, ultimately, the historic Western

> confusion about the relation between art and morality, the aesthetic and the ethical.
>
> For the problem of art versus morality is a pseudo problem. The distinction itself is a trap; its continued plausibility rests on not putting the ethical into question, but only the aesthetic. To argue on these grounds at all, seeking to defend the autonomy of art...is already to grant something that should not be granted—namely, that there exist two independent sorts of response, the aesthetic and the ethical, which vie for our loyalty when we experience a work of art. As if during the experience one really had to choose between responsible and humane conduct, on the one hand, and the pleasurable stimulation of consciousness, on the other!

Much of Sontag's essay is concerned to break down the opposition between "style" and "content," but unlike others who sometimes complain about the persistence of this opposition but do so mostly in order to banish "style" from critical discussion altogether—it's just the writer's way of communicating his/her content—Sontag maintains it is content that should recede, becoming simply the word for a "special stylistic convention." Style is the real substance of art, content its outer decoration, the enticement to the reader's attention that allows the "experience" of art that style enables.

Sontag was unfortunately denied her wish that critical theory might move "to examine in detail the formal function of subject-matter." Academic criticism has gone in precisely the opposite direction, dismissing form altogether in order to focus on the "subject-matter" that satisfies the critic's pre-established theoretical disposition, while there's very little "critical theory" at all in general-interest publications of the sort that once published writers like Susan Sontag. Essentially, the debate over the fraught relationship between "style" and "content" is about where Sontag left it.

Unfortunately, she left it presumably resolved to her own satisfaction, but not in a way that satisfies any current attempt to advance the argument that "style is on the inside." Since the notion that subject-matter is mostly a formal function seems if anything more outlandish even than it must have in 1965, a case needs to be made for it that extends beyond Sontag's somewhat idiosyncratic account and that avoids what I consider her more serious missteps.

The most serious problem with "On Style," in my opinion, is that Sontag can't finally unburden her argument of the criticisms of aestheticism made by the moralists she otherwise castigates. It seems to me her observation that it is quite easy to keep separate "responsible and humane conduct" from "the pleasurable stimulation of consciousness" without the latter contaminating the former would entirely suffice as a rebuttal of these criticisms, but she spends a great deal of her essay—the heart of it, really—defending the notion that art should not be judged by the standard of "humane conduct" since art and the experience of art are phenomena of "consciousness," not actions requiring moral scrutiny. In fact, immediately after making the observation she begins to back off, assuring skeptics that "Of course, we never have a purely aesthetic response to works of art—neither to a play or a novel, with its depicting of human beings choosing and acting, nor, though it is less obvious, to a painting by Jackson Pollack or a Greek vase."

Since we never have a "pure" response to anything, I can't see that this proviso is necessary. If it isn't obvious to readers that a depiction of "human beings choosing and acting" is not the same thing as human beings choosing and acting, and that it would be irrational "for us to make a moral response to something in a work of art in the same sense that we do to an act in real life," then any further attempt to heighten those readers' aesthetic awareness isn't going to accomplish much, anyway. Although Sontag argues that "we can in good conscience cherish works of art which, considered in terms of 'content,' are morally objectionable" (her brief defense of Leni Riefenstahl's documentaries is the best-known illustration of this possibility), finally she can't let "morality" go as an issue relevant to the creation and experience of art. "Art is connected with morality," she asserts. "The moral pleasure in art, as well as the moral service that art performs, consists in the intelligent gratification of consciousness."

Much is elided in that formulation "intelligent gratification." Is "unintelligent" gratification immoral, or just lack of artistry? Is lack of artistry itself a moral issue, or simply a critical/evaluative judgment? Does only the greatest art perform the "moral service" Sontag associates with the "intelligent gratification of consciousness"? I don't object to the formulation itself—John Dewey would probably have found it usefully synonymous with his own notion of "art as experience"—but to insist that it must have a moral dimension seems to undo almost completely Sontag's case—which she admits she has made "uneasily"—for the autonomy of art:

> But if we understand morality in the singular, as a generic decision on the part of consciousness, then it appears that our response to art is "moral" insofar as it is, precisely, the enlivening of our sensibility and consciousness. For it is sensibility that nourishes our capacity for moral choice, and prompts our readiness to act, assuming that we do choose, which is a prerequisite for calling an act moral, and are not just blindly and unreflectingly obeying. Art performs this "moral" task because the qualities which are intrinsic to the aesthetic experience (disinterestedness, contemplativeness, attentiveness, the awakening of the feelings) and to the aesthetic object (grace, intelligence, expressiveness, energy, sensuousness) are also fundamental constituents of a moral response to life.

Again, there isn't much here with which I would fundamentally disagree, but Sontag comes close to suggesting that art needs this moral justification, that "contemplativeness" and "attentiveness" are not in themselves sufficiently desirable qualities. They are "moral" insofar as they are good things to exercise, but I can't see that an explicit justification of them—and thus of aesthetic experience itself—on moral grounds is otherwise relevant. Either art needs no moral justification to strengthen its appeal or it is an impetus to moral action after all. Sontag wants to believe the first, but really seems to believe the second.

At the center of Sontag's discussion of style in "On Style" is her emphasis on the role of "will" in the creation and reception of art:

Perhaps the best way of clarifying the nature of our experience of works of art, and the relation between art and the rest of human feeling and doing, is to invoke the notion of will. It is a useful notion because will is not just a particular posture of consciousness, energized consciousness. It is also an attitude toward the world, of a subject toward the world.

The complex kind of willing that is embodied, and communicated, in a work of art both abolishes the world and encounters it in an extraordinarily intense and specialized way. This double aspect of the will in art is succinctly expressed by [Raymond] Bayer when he says: "Each work of art gives us the schematized and disengaged memory of a volition." Insofar as it schematized, disengaged, a memory, the willing involved in art sets itself at a distance from the world. . . .

Art must distance itself from the world in order to become visible as art in the first place. It comes into being as a version of the world, as an aesthetic reproduction, and for this to be accomplished as thoroughly as is necessary, both for artist and audience, an act of "will" is required. And this act could be described as "dehumanized," since

> in order to appear to us as art, the work must restrict sentimental intervention and emotional participation, which are functions of "closeness." It is the degree and manipulating of this distance, the conventions of distance, which constitute the style of the work.

Although I really don't understand how this effort of aesthetic willing could itself be identified as a work's "style" (more on this below), otherwise the concept of "will" as the imposition of a purely formal status on a text, image, or soundscape seems a cogent enough formulation. Most readers of novels, viewers of paintings or sculpture, and listeners to music want to disregard art's distancing effects and recover a notional "closeness" Sontag duly reminds us is antithetical to the very creation of art.

But again Sontag can't seem to accept the full implications of her position. She must add a codicil:

> A work of art is first of all an object, not an imitation; and it is true that all great art is founded on distance, on artificiality, on style, on what Ortega [y Gasset] calls dehumanization. But the notion of distance, (and of dehumanization, as well) is misleading, unless one adds that the movement is not just away from but toward the world. The overcoming or transcending of the world in art is also a way of encountering the world, and of training or educating the will to be in the world. . . .

This encountering of the world is what Sontag calls the "function" of art, which she thus substitutes for "content" in opposition to the art "object." She appears to believe that in so doing she is banishing "content" as a subject of critical discussion, but I can't really see how "function" operates as any less of an obstacle to the appreciation of style—which for Sontag remains the only "substance" of art—as the content it effectively displaces. If previously a work of art could be judged by the moral or social ramifications of its "content," what, under Sontag's formulation of "function," would prevent it from being judged by how acceptably it performs the task of "educating the will to be in the world"? Art would still be valued at least as much—probably, inevitably, more—for its utilitarian intervention in "the world" as it would as a self-sufficient creation, an act of aesthetic will.

The function of a work of art is to be itself. It doesn't engage in "training" for anything other than subsequent, perhaps more "educated" experiences of art. No doubt some people regard some works of art as having provided them the kind of enhanced re-engagement with the world of "real" experience that Sontag invokes—keeping in mind that works of art themselves belong to the world of experience—but to posit that art has a function that makes it useful to the world for reasons other than being available to experience, and this function applies at all times for all people, only gives away to the philistines what Sontag otherwise seems to want to preserve—the integrity of art.

Part of the reason for Sontag's readiness to trade "object" for "function" may lie in the ultimate imprecision of her notion of "style" in art, especially as style is embodied in works of literature: "Style is the principle of decision in a work of art, the signature of the artist's will"; "If art is the supreme game which the will plays with itself, 'style' consists of the set of rules by which the game is played"; "To the extent that a work seems right, just, unimaginable otherwise (without loss or damage), what we are responding to is a quality of its style"; "An artist's style is, from a technical point of view, nothing other than the particular idiom in which he deploys the forms of his art"; "[E]very style embodies an epistemological decision, an interpretation of how and what we see." Nowhere in "On Style" is there discussion of color or brushstroke, tone or harmonics, phrases, sentences, or paragraphs. "Particular idiom" in poetry or fiction is never associated with specific effects of language, with the use of words.

The closest Sontag comes to a real analysis of style is this brief discussion of Gertrude Stein:

> The circular repetitive style of Gertrude Stein's *Melanctha* expresses her interest in the dilution of immediate awareness by memory and anticipation, what she calls "association," which is obscured in language by the system of the tenses. Stein's insistence on the presentness of experience is identical with her decision to keep to the present tense, to choose commonplace short words and repeat groups of them incessantly, to use an extremely loose syntax and abjure most punctuation. Every style is a means of insisting on something.

It would be hard not to notice Stein's "circular repetitive style"—her particular idiom of "commonplace short words" and "extremely loose syntax"—but this sort of focus on style as the deployment of language is relevant to all writers worth our notice, and otherwise "On Style" defines style much more abstractly as "principle of decision," "set of rules," and "epistemological decision." And even here Stein's prose style is summed up as an aspect of will, as the "means of insisting on something," rather than as the enlistment of words in an aesthetically compelling verbal composition. A writer's "style" can be examined for its successes and failures in meeting the latter goal; as an embodiment of "will" it remains, for me at least, rather too mistily metaphysical.

On the other hand, Sontag seems correct to me when she concludes the essay by reminding us that "In the strictest sense, all the contents of consciousness are ineffable," that "Every work of art, therefore, needs to be understood not only as something rendered, but also as a certain handling of the ineffable."

> In the greatest art, one is always aware of things that cannot be said. . ., of the contradiction between expression and the presence of the inexpressible. Stylistic devices are also techniques of avoidance. The most potent elements in a work of art are, often, its silences.

I would only add that the "silences" cultivated by great art are "present" because the work makes room for them in a concrete way. They are incorporated into the work as "ineffable" but real. (The New Critics might have called this ineffable quality "ambiguity," something half-said but not fully said.) The specific way in which, through its style, the work of art invokes a fruitful silence is always still worth attention.

Harold Bloom

*N*ot far into *The Anatomy of Influence*, Harold Bloom provides what attentive readers could consider an explanation of sorts for his curious status in both the general literary culture and among academic critics. "More than a half a century as a teacher," he writes, "has shown me that I am best as a provocation for my students, a realization that has carried over into my writing. That stance alienates some readers in the media and in the academy, but they are not my audience."

There is no doubt that Bloom has proven to be a "provocation" beyond the classroom, and in a way that often "alienates" rather than productively challenges, which is no doubt the effect Bloom hopes to have on his students. Most recently Bloom has provoked the "media" to purvey an image of him as an elitist, curmudgeonly defender of tradition and scourge of the popular, a literary dinosaur still roaming the earth even though the climate in which he finds himself has irreversibly shifted. Bloom thus seems to appear to some "ordinary" readers as a rather menacing figure whose views stand as a challenge to their reading habits, or as a rather pompously comic figure whose opinions can be safely dismissed. Bloom himself actually anticipates this latter response to his books in his frequent self-identification with Sir John Falstaff, although it is Falstaff's refusal to be anything other than himself that Bloom most prizes.

But if Bloom has alienated literary journalists and casual readers by his willingness to make distinctions and to assert literature's seriousness of purpose, before his current incarnation as a kind of public critic he also alienated his original scholarly audience as well, although for a time he was considered not an apostate from academic criticism but among its most cutting-edge practitioners. While today Bloom is perceived as an enemy of "theory," during the 1970s he was himself a prominent, even notorious, theorist whose Freudian-based account of poetic influence scandalized his more traditional colleagues and even led to his being grouped with radical theorists such as Derrida, de Man, and Foucault. Eventually it became clear that Bloom's invocation of Freud and Nietzsche was part of an attempt to account for the power of great works of literature, not to diminish their value, and Bloom gradually began to provoke the scorn of "advanced" critical theorists, a scorn he freely returned by dubbing them members of the "school of resentment."

So if the book reviewers and the academic critics no longer represent Bloom's audience, who is his audience? One could uncharitably conclude that Bloom constitutes his own audience of one, but the very fact that he turned to a "popularizing" approach to both literature and his own ideas about literature and that he has now produced what he calls "my virtual swan song, my [attempt] to say in one place most of what I have learned about how influence works in imaginative literature" suggests that he does want to reach potentially sympathetic readers outside the academy, who might still be persuaded by the depth of his commitment to poetry (understood as the primal source of all "literature") and his understanding of literary history to value great poetry more highly—if not as passionately as Bloom himself (which might be impossible), then more than both the culture at large and academic literary study currently allows. That Bloom does emphasize "great" works of literature perhaps seems hopelessly old-fashioned, an attempt to prop up one of the pillars of Western culture, but finally Bloom is less interested in celebrating greatness per se, whether in people or in civilization, than he is in conveying to the reader the power of poetry at its most vital.

Bloom signals in *The Anatomy of Influence* an awareness of the ways in which his previous books have been misunderstood, if not deliberately misconstrued, and thus the first chapter of the book attempts to clarify what Bloom has actually written in such books as *The Anxiety of Influence* and *Agon*. Perhaps the most serious misconception about Bloom's theory of "influence" is that influence is something tangibly felt by a writer through his/her consciousness of a precursor writer acting as inspiration. But as Bloom points out, "Influence anxiety exists between poems and not between persons." While in some cases a poet might be aware of this anxiety "at whatever level of consciousness," for the literary critic "all that matters is the revisionary relationship between poems, as manifested in tropes, images, diction, syntax, grammar, metric, poetic stance." One could say that Bloom's approach to the reading of poetry requires both close attention to the text—looking for the tropes, images, etc.—and an awareness of literary history, the ways in which the poem's manifest qualities maintain a connection, however much the poem seeks its own autonomy, with the poems that have already been written and that inevitably prompted, directly and indirectly, the new poem. "Poetic thought is always a mode of memory," writes Bloom. "Primarily this is the memory of prior poems."

Bloom's approach thus diverges from that of the New Critics, against whom Bloom was reacting in his critical work of the 1960s and '70s, whose too-exclusive focus on "the tropes, the images, and the diction" for Bloom inappropriately separated the individual poem from "poetry." One cannot sufficiently appeal to the former without also appreciating its place in the development of the latter, since the poem will always be marked by the "anxiety" produced by the unavoidable operation of influence. In *The Anxiety of Influence*, Bloom called for "a wholly different practical criticism" than conventional close reading, one that gave up "the failed enterprise of seeking to 'understand' any single poem as an entity in itself":

> Let us pursue instead the quest of learning to read any poem as its poet's deliberate misinterpretation, as a poet, of a precursor poem or poetry in general.

The Anatomy of Influence is also an attempt to clear up misapprehensions of what Bloom intends by such a formulation as "deliberate misinterpretation." Bloom's own notion of the "misreading" has itself been misread, even deliberately, but this is merely a "weak" misreading that is simply a matter of getting Bloom wrong. A strong misreading is a "creative" one, indeed where poetry is concerned it is the very fountainhead of creativity. It is a type of defense mechanism whereby the poet (as what Bloom calls an "ephebe," a poet-in-the-making) wards off the potentially debilitating power of the precursor by "swerving" away into a new expression or stance. In a sense the poet's misreading is also "wrong," but because of the nature of literature as a form of expression, there can finally be no wrong reading by a strong poet or critic:

> . . . correct readings are not possible if a literary work is sublime enough. A correct reading merely would repeat the text, while asserting that it speaks for itself. It does not. The more powerful a literary artifice, the more it relies upon figurative language.

"Misreading" does not mean mischaracterizing or misidentifying a text's proper meaning, since there is no proper meaning to strong works of literature. It is a figurative transformation of a "discourse" that is itself inescapably figurative.

Misreadings of Bloom, to the extent they are not simply willful attempts to distort what he means, represent a failure to understand that for Bloom criticism is also unavoidably a "resort to figuration." How could the effort to comprehend "highly figurative language" be anything but figurative, unless it is outright an attempt to tame it, to restate it in other, inevitably reductive, terms? (If the poem could be expressed that way, why wasn't it?) "To practice criticism," according to Bloom, "is to think poetically about poetic thinking." Thus those who expect that Bloom will match his privileging of the aesthetic qualities of literature with systematic, detailed close readings of individual texts are perhaps disappointed to find instead what can seem like generalizations or simply Bloom's own passionately expressed appreciations. Those unprepared for Bloom's "figurative" style of criticism perhaps take his formulations too literally, or don't understand his excursions into Jewish mysticism or classical authors. To the extent that his erudite and declamatory method causes misunderstanding, *The Anatomy of Influence* does arguably work best as a summing-up and a corrective.

Bloom is probably perceived by some casual readers as dauntingly "serious," and *The Anatomy of Influence* might help to correct the mistaken assumption not so much that Bloom does take literature seriously (the book's subtitle, "Literature as a Way of Life" unequivocally signals this fact), but why he does so. Bloom is no moralist or academic taskmaster, certain that reading great books is good for us. While he does often identify with Samuel Johnson, a stern moral critic if there ever was one, as Bloom tells us in a brief chapter on Johnson's critical influence, "Johnson as a literary critic means most to me in his apprehension of Shakespeare," whose centrality to the Western literary tradition is made emphatically clear throughout *The Anatomy of Influence*. (In many ways the influence of Johnson on Bloom is the latter's own creative misreading, reaching for the "Romantic strain" in Johnson that values imagination over "stability.") Bloom expresses only disdain for Matthew Arnold, the other great moral critic, whose reasons for advocating a Western canon are not Bloom's.

Although he professes devotion to Johnson, Bloom's stronger alliance is to Walter Pater. "As a disciple of Walter Pater and his ephebe Oscar Wilde," he confesses, "I am an Epicurean literary critic, reliant upon sensations, perceptions, and impressions." Bloom values Shakespeare because he so capaciously provides these sensations and impressions, giving us access to the "sublime," which is Bloom's highest measure of aesthetic success. He follows Pater in regarding the sublime "as the adding of strangeness to beauty." Bloom further associates strangeness with "uncanniness," which is the "estrangement of the homelike or commonplace." Shakespeare is the most distinguished creator of the sublime in literature:

> Shakespeare, when you give yourself completely to reading him, surprises you by the strangeness which I take to be his salient quality. We feel the consciousness of Hamlet or Iago, and our own consciousness strangely expands. The difference between reading Shakespeare and reading nearly any other writer is that greater widening of our consciousness into what initially must seem a strangeness of woe or wonder.

If Shakespeare or any of the other writers Bloom discusses in *The Anatomy of Influence* are good for us it is because of this "widening of consciousness," not because they instruct or enlighten us. The sublime is a form of pleasure, although it is a "difficult pleasure," one that can prompt both "woe" and "wonder," or a complex intermingling of the two. It may thus give rise to the closest facsimile of an authentic religious experience, at least for Bloom, who otherwise professes no religious belief, his attachment to the Jewish tradition notwithstanding. Those of us who are willing to follow Bloom through his version of the canon and the anxieties of influence that bring it into being, his invocations of Kabbalah and Longinus, his insistence on "misreading" as the source of innovation, and his sometimes oracular pronouncements and judgments because his commitment to the value and integrity of literature is so palpable and his insights are indeed so provocative perhaps at this point might begin to resist Bloom's outlook as excessively metaphysical, a private perspective that provides Bloom with a "way of life" the rest of us can't really share.

Such resistance to the intensity of Bloom's search for the sublime may provide the most cogent explanation of the accusation he is a "snob." For Bloom, literature offers the truest access to the widening of consciousness he seeks, and books he judges do not promise such access are simply not worth taking seriously. And Bloom has seemingly so narrowed the range of works he does take seriously, and employs such arcane means of finding their value, he leaves the impression only he knows how to find it, that the canon he celebrates belongs to him. Even though an acquaintance with the numerous volumes of essays on various authors and works Bloom has edited (the Chelsea House series) will demonstrate that his approbation extends to many more writers than his reputation as a critical taskmaster would suggest, nevertheless he perhaps unavoidably cuts a somewhat embarrassing figure in an era when taking literature seriously is often seen as an offense to the democratic equality of taste, if not outright complicity with a legacy of cultural imperialism.

The Anatomy of Influence is not likely to alter this perception among those who temperamentally could never take literature seriously because they take nothing seriously, or those for whom it is too frivolous to be taken seriously, but there ought to be readers in the sizable group fitting neither of these descriptions who could separate the ponderous manner Bloom at times affects in defense of what he fears are besieged literary values from potentially valid descriptions of the process of literary influence and of what precisely is original in the work of the writers Bloom examines and thus justifies their inclusion in the canon. If close reading is not always Bloom's chosen avenue of approach to these writers, the extended, bravura analysis of, for example, Hart Crane's *The Bridge* just might convert readers to Bloom's view that Crane is an unjustly overlooked poet, and his discussion of the influence of *Hamlet* on Milton's *Paradise Lost* might itself convince the reader the "anxiety of influence" is real.

The book as well is structured in a way that clarifies the line of descent of influence in both English and American poetry. The numerous chapters devoted to Shakespeare recapitulates many of the essential points Bloom made in *Shakespeare: The Invention of the Human*, but they also allow him to delineate Shakespeare's influence on subsequent poets from Milton to Yeats, while his extended discussion of Walt Whitman allows him to do the same thing with the American poets who follow Whitman. Readers should get from *The Anatomy of Influence* an encompassing perspective on English language literary history (with a few detours into other languages as well) that provides the opportunity to assess whether Bloom's account of how a tradition establishes and perpetuates itself seems convincing. Since any particular poem or any particular poet can acquire full significance only from within such a tradition, the book also could be said to offer a final statement of a theory of how poetry gets written. This may ultimately be the most important contribution Harold Bloom has made to the study of literature, and *The Anatomy of Influence* is if nothing else a useful condensation of Bloom's exploration of the source of "poetic thinking."

Readers who do find what Bloom has to say in *The Anatomy of Influence* worth contemplating will still want to move from it to *The Anxiety of Influence*, which remains arguably the most powerful version of the theory. Whereas in the new book Bloom announces that, in a critical climate he calls the "New Cynicism," he wants to modify his conception of the anxiety of influence by redefining it as "literary love, tempered by defense," in the first book he is willing to emphasize the more direful aspects of the poet's struggle for expression in the shadow of the precursor poet. "If the imagination's gift comes necessarily from the perversity of the spirit," he writes there,

> then the living labyrinth of literature is built upon the ruin of every impulse most generous in us. So apparently it is and must be—we are wrong to have founded a humanism directly upon literature itself, and the phrase "humane letters" is an oxymoron. A humanism might still be founded on a completer study of literature than we have yet achieved, but never upon literature itself....

If all writers are in a sense indebted to other writers through influence, it is not the sort of influence that would lead the best of them to feel part of a "community":

> It does happen that one poet influences another, or more precisely, that one poet's poems influence the poems of the other, through a generosity of the spirit, even a shared generosity. But our easy idealism is out of place here. Where generosity is involved, the poets influenced are minor or weaker; the more generosity, and the more mutual it is, the poorer the poets involved.

In *The Anatomy of Influence* Bloom somewhat softens this appeal to the self-centered, exclusionary forces (both Freudian and Nietzschean) that contribute to acts of true creativity, but it seems unlikely through his notion of "literary love" he now intends to suggest that the poetic impulse is a beneficent and convivial one after all. However, what Bloom really seems to reject is not the belief that literature represents a supreme human achievement but the "idealism" that would overlook the struggle involved or assume that the purpose of poetry is to benefit "humanity" in general. As Bloom indicates, it is possible to conduct through the study of literature an activity that is "humane" in its ambition, but this would have to be a literary study that does not distort or deny the source of literature in the depths of the "perverse" persistence of the human imagination.

Bloom's engagement with both poetry and poems occurs most vitally in the depths of imaginative expression, his Paterian inclination toward "sensations" notwithstanding. In *The Anatomy of Influence* he reinforces his view that influence "works in the depths of image and idea, and produces intricate evasions that nevertheless bud and bloom." It is "at its deepest . . . remote from echo and allusion, though it does not exclude them," and is not primarily "an affair of stylistics." As someone who belongs to that group of readers who willingly forms the audience for Harold Bloom's provocations, I here find myself provoked to my own strongest objection to Bloom's critical method. While a focus on "image and idea" does not "exclude" attention to style, in general to the surface features of a literary text, Bloom's preoccupation with the "deep" and to some extent impalpable elements of the text too easily dismisses the relevance of "stylistics" in the experience of literature, even in determining the nature of "influence."

If influence can only be traced "between poems," it seems somewhat arbitrary to assume it can be discerned more readily in those qualities of the poem that are to an extent invisible than in those that are manifestly visible.

Harold Bloom is in many ways a model of the literary critic urging readers to pay close attention to the works of literature we read. But for Bloom this attention is not first directed at the formal or stylistic features that we would immediately regard as "aesthetic." Those features are in a sense taken for granted by Bloom, even as it is the aesthetic power of the poem that makes available the "deeper" content he is after. Reading for content is of course a common enough practice, even among literary critics, but ultimately Bloom's pursuit of the evidence of influence as he understands it does threaten to become a Quixotic one (not that Bloom would necessarily consider this an unflattering description), the object of the pursuit to seem an esoteric one the importance of which is paramount primarily to Harold Bloom. There is still much to be learned from Bloom's provocations, but probably his kind of reading can't really be done by anyone else.

≈

Richard Poirier

*A*s I was working on a dissertation that was conspicuously about "postmodern" fiction, examined from a "poststructuralist" perspective, several of my readers expressed surprise at my extensive citation of Richard Poirier's 1966 book, *A World Elsewhere: The Place of Style in American Literature*. Although in my opinion this book is one of the most important academic studies of American literature, it had at that time become somewhat neglected even among "Americanist" scholars, but this was not the only reason readers found its prominence in my dissertation a little strange. What they really saw as unexpected was the extent to which supposedly postmodern and poststructuralist ideas about language and literary form could be discovered in Poirier's book, written well before either of these terms were much in circulation and well before critical theory became the dominant approach to literary study. I now think that perhaps the main reason *A World Elsewhere* had fallen into some obscurity was precisely that it offered a radical analysis of American literature and literary history.

A World Elsewhere makes it clear that American literature has long been characterized by a preoccupation with the processes of representation and specifically with the limitations of language as a medium of representation, features generally associated with postmodernism and assumed to be a phenomenon of more recent literary history. Such a view of American literary history was implicitly unsettling to the prevailing approach to the study of American literature, which emphasized literature as a reflection of American history, often embodying "themes" said to be the obsessions of American writers in their encounter with history and culture. But Poirier in *A World Elsewhere* tells us that most of the canonical American writers distrust the very mechanisms available to poets and fiction writers that would render experience adequately, and if anything they aspire to write in such a way that they manage to escape history. "The great works of American literature," he writes, "are alive with the effort to stabilize certain feelings and attitudes that have, as it were, no place in the world, no place at all except where a writer's style can give them one." Thus these great works lead us not to the world of historical experience but to "a world elsewhere."

Poirier's insights arise mostly from an analysis of 19th century fiction (although Faulkner receives significant attention as well), but they are equally relevant to an understanding of the seemingly extravagant qualities of much unconventional post-World War II American fiction, or at least so I contended in my own study of metafiction (which was in its initial incarnation an American phenomenon). I took Poirier's claims even a little farther, arguing that the self-reflexivity of metafiction, in directing the reader's attention to the artifice of language, in effect makes style itself the "world elsewhere," asking the reader not to regard language as the transparent medium for the invocation of a created "world" at all but as fiction's primary source of interest, the irreducible substance of the reading experience. Along with the American writer's propensity to favor "romance" over "novel" (a distinction made by Hawthorne), this emphasis on style (really an insistence that a work of fiction is finally a construction of words) helps to explain why American fiction has long seemed peculiarly "other" in comparison to British and European fiction—a difference that is often enough taken as a sign of inferiority but has actually made American fiction inherently "experimental" throughout its history.

Poirier's reading of American fiction (and poetry as well) was directly inspired by his primary reading of Emerson, as illustrated especially in his 1987 book, *The Renewal of Literature*. In my opinion, Poirier is the indispensable commentator on Emerson—certainly few other critics are able to do equal justice to Emerson the philosopher and Emerson the writer as thoroughly as Poirier. He identifies Emerson, correctly in my view, as not just the source of "American" ideas and attitudes that are echoed in many other writers (whether they are always aware of it or not), but of the quintessentially American approach to style as well. For anyone who has found Emerson's ideas interesting enough in the abstract but difficult to track as expressed through his aphoristic, circuitous prose style, Poirier's account of Emerson the writer can be revelatory. Emerson feared above all "being caught or fixed in a meaning" or "state of conformity," Poirier contends, and that fear is addressed first of all in Emerson's own deployment of language. Thus Emerson's prose is perhaps the supreme example of the centrality of "troping" in American literature, the "turning" of language in new or surprising ways that allow the writer (and the reader) to avoid being trapped in established usages and forms. In this way Emerson's writing doesn't so much "develop" through sequential discourse, which relies on already accepted patterns of thought, as it continually "transitions" from one formulation of language to another. "Emerson makes himself sometimes amazingly hard to read," writes Poirier,

> hard to get close to, all the more because he finds it manifestly difficult to get close to himself, to read or understand himself. If you want to get to know him, you must stay as close as possible to the movements of his language, moment by moment, for at every moment there is movement with no

place to rest; you must share, to a degree few other writers since Shakespeare have asked us to do, in his contentions with his own and therefore with our own meanings, as these pass into and then out of any particular verbal configuration.

Emerson's essays do not present finished thoughts but illustrate a process of thinking. In purely literary terms, they are examples of writing that displays a "thoroughgoing inquisitiveness about its own verbal resources, let[ting] itself discover as much as can be known about the previous uses of its words." For Poirier, a work of literature "can be of lasting interest only if it reveals" such inquisitiveness. This view of the "literary" also leads to Poirier's conception of the role of criticism. Although he was not a New Critic, he explains the preponderance of close reading in *The Renewal of Literature* as the result of his belief that "criticism should engage itself not with rendered experience but the experience of rendering; it must go back to acts of rendition in language." Almost all of Poirier's criticism (of literature at least, since he also occasionally examined other forms, such as in his rather famous essay on The Beatles) is intensively focused on textual analysis, and few critics demonstrate the value of attending closely to the words of the text as does Poirier in his efforts to disclose those "verbal resources" the writer has engaged, as in this analysis of Robert Frost's "Mending Wall":

> . . . The sound of the opening line of the poem, "Something there is that doesn't love a wall," creates a mystery, or what the poem itself calls a "gap." This gap is not filled by summary bits of wisdom, like "good fences make good neighbors," a line given, it should be remembered, to "an old-stone savage armed," as if aphorisms are crude weaponry. No, good neighbors are made by phrases whose incompleteness is the very sign of neighborliness: "something there is." Anyone can go along with that. The word "something" partakes mildly of the "mischief" attributed to the emergent energies of spring, when the frozen ground swell "makes gaps even two can pass abreast." It is the sort of "mischief" which creates

chances for companionability; this "something" doesn't love walls; its love is given instead to the "gaps" in walls wherein people may join.

Poirier was concerned to read literary texts with such attentiveness because the writers he most admired were themselves so constantly attentive to the figurations of language. At the same time that Poirier's readings help elucidate the tangible qualities of these works and thus enhance our own reading of them, his analyses also center on identifying the way in which such features arise from an orientation to language Poirier calls "linguistic skepticism." Poirier considers linguistic skepticism to be the literary expression of American pragmatism, an association he pursues most directly in the 1992 book, *Poetry and Pragmatism*. Much of this book is devoted to discussions of William James and, again, Emerson, although Poirier makes a convincing case that it is Emerson who is truly the inspiration for the philosophical orientation James will ultimately label "pragmatism." Emerson's emphases on action and individual agency and his distrust of inherited systems are direct influences on both James and John Dewey, but it is in the manifestation of these beliefs in Emerson's approach to language and in his habits of writing that he initiates a "pragmatic tradition" in American literature, one that Poirier assigns figuratively to "poetry" but which includes both poets and novelists, as well as essayists such as Emerson and Thoreau.

Writers in this tradition are especially aware of the contingency of language, its unavoidable immersion in past practices and ultimately its insufficiency as a medium for establishing the final truth of things. They understand that, in Poirier's words, the "proper activity" of all writers is "essentially a poetic one. It is to make sure that language is kept in a state of continuous troping, turning, transforming, transfiguring. . . ." The act of writing is thus alive with the attempt to "stabilize certain feelings and attitudes," but the attempt itself provides the only stability, and it will of course be "turned" by subsequent attempts, the transfiguration it accomplishes achieving, in Robert Frost's famous words, only "a momentary stay against confusion."

Poirier believes, as do I, that this "momentary stay" is "quite enough," but I also think that, if there is a limitation to Poirier's critical project, it would be his (not to mention Emerson's) underemphasis on the aesthetic satisfaction a work of literature might still provide well beyond the "momentary" act of troping. However much Emerson urges that the poetic impulse is "continuous," never resting in any particular expression, poems, stories, and novels retain the capacity to provoke an aesthetic experience for potential readers. If the greatest works do not necessarily bear comparison to the "well-wrought urn" in their manifest aesthetic qualities, those qualities are real and are the most immediate object of the experience of literature, unless poetry and fiction differ from more straightforward forms of discourse only in being less direct in communicating "meaning." In his focus on style, Poirier certainly does not reduce the work of literature to its interpreted meaning, but it nevertheless does seem to me that a pragmatic criticism, or a study of the pragmatic strain in American literature, could allow for the way style interacts with form and for the way their interaction in a particular text can produce literary art of more or less enduring value.

Poirier quite rightly points out that Emersonian pragmatism has always been in its anti-foundationalism "postmodern." But Poirier also helps us understand that the writers influenced by Emerson do not despair at the contingency of language or abandon all purpose because truth will always remain elusive. Instead, they proceed according to the belief that, as Poirier puts it, "language, and therefore thinking, can be changed by an individual's acts of imagination and by an individual's manipulation of words." "Manipulation of words" is finally what literature is about, and ultimately the change in thinking such manipulation can effect is a change in the disposition of words, a fresh appreciation of the "transfiguring" power of words. Arguably, Poirier's greatest contribution to literature and literary criticism was to show us why playing "word games" does not trivialize the writer's vocation, as some readers and critics seem to think, but is in fact the essence of that vocation, the most serious ambition a writer can possess.

Richard Poirier was an exemplary "academic critic" of a kind no longer much in evidence, one who combined formidable learning with an impeccable literary sensibility and who regarded academic criticism as a useful complement to literature—a study that attempted to deepen our apprehension of literature, not to affect a scholarly superiority to it. "Reading is nothing if not personal," he wrote in an especially Emersonian mode in *Poetry and Pragmatism*. "It ought to get down ultimately to a struggle between what you want to make of a text and what it wants to make of itself and of you." These days literary scholars are preoccupied with "what you want to make of a text," mostly dismissing "what it wants to make of itself" and ignoring "what it wants to make of you." Poirier could acknowledge the limitations of criticism, maintaining that "skepticism needs also to be directed at the language of criticism itself and its claims to large significance." Those claims by academic critics have become only more inflated, and unfortunately there are now few critics like Richard Poirier around to return us to the significance implicit in the reading experience itself, where the reader's struggle to make the most of the text mirrors the writer's struggle to allow language to make what sense it can.

William Gass

William Gass has often been praised as an essayist (perhaps more often than as a fiction writer), but for the most part Gass's essays are more appropriately regarded as literary criticism. However, Gass is generally not concerned with making and justifying judgments about the superior and inferior in works of literature (although judgment is always implicit) but with carefully, and, in his singular, sinuous style, insightfully explicating those features of the texts and authors he admires that will help other readers share his admiration. At other times his essays are essentially exercises in aesthetics, although the aesthetic explorations are always grounded in specific practices or specific writers. Few literary critics are able to combine deep erudition, critical discernment, and a keen aesthetic sensibility as does Gass, and few offer readers such an opportunity to enlarge their own understanding of and sensitivity to expressions of literary art.

To a degree, Gass's criticism seems an extension of his work as a fiction writer, a critical elaboration of the assumptions underlying it and the methods animating it. But Gass's critical impulses are too generous and his focus too thoroughly on the dynamics of literary creation in general for his essays to be taken as a collective apology for his own style-centered, formally audacious fiction—although certainly it does provide critical support for that sort of aesthetically challenging writing, both in fiction and in poetry. Moreover, in Gass's readings, "aesthetically challenging" is more or less identical with the "aesthetic" per se, so that in describing and delighting in the writers who are the subjects of many of the essays, and in contemplating the devices and strategies available to the literary artist, Gass has been engaged in a lifelong project of alerting us to the presence of aesthetic beauty, however "difficult" or unconventional. He is one of those critics, in fact, who has endeavored to keep the very notion of aesthetic beauty alive at a time when it is often viewed with skepticism as "snobbery" or "elitism."

Gass is not a snob, although he may be an elitist, but only in the sense, as he puts it in "The Test of Time," that he belongs to the "unorganized few. . .who sincerely love the arts." He—and those of us who would like to be there with him—does not declare allegiance to this group because the arts make us better people or superior people or more refined people but because what they provide is good in itself: "There are those for whom reading, for example, can be an act of love, and lead to a revelation, not of truth, moral or otherwise, but of lucidity, order, rightness of relation, the experience of a world fully felt and furnished." If great works of art and literature "teach" us anything, they teach us "immersion." For Gass, "they teach me that the trivial is as important as the important when looked at importantly."

"The arts" in their individual forms thus are worthy of attention when they can be "looked at importantly" through an immersion in their well-wrought particulars. In "The Test of Time," Gass focuses on two writers, seemingly very different kinds of writers, but who both nevertheless enlarge our perceptions through their renderings with words. In *Walden*, Thoreau perpetually brings the pond and his experiences there to life:

> . . .we, as readers, are not brought to Walden Pond in some poetic time machine. We experience Walden as it passed through Thoreau's head, his whole heart there for us to pass through, too, his wide bright eyes the better to see with, the patient putting together of his prose to appreciate. Of the pond, the trees, the pain, the poet may retain—through the indelibilities of his medium—moments which, in reality, went as swiftly as a whistle away; but he will also give them what was never there in the first place: much afterthought, correction, suggestion, verbal movement, emotion, meaning, music. . . .

Gerard Manley Hopkins would seem to be the more obviously suited to Gass's aesthetic ideal rooted in detail and sensuous sound, and indeed he is valued for these qualities, even as they failed to satisfy Hopkins himself: In poetically brooding over whether there is a way "to keep back beauty. . .from vanishing away," Hopkins, writes Gass, "said it was 'yonder,' in effect, up high in the air, as 'high as that,' when all the while he knew where it was: it was there under his forming fingers; it was in his writing, where the real god, the god he could not avow—dared not worship—worked, wrote, writing his rhetorical regrets, putting his question so perfectly the proof was in the putting." In Hopkins's poetry:

> They, those things, the terrible sonnets, every one, were composed, brought by Hopkins into being, not when he was down in the dumps, not while he was Hopkins, but when he was a Poet, truly on top of the world, the muse his mother; and the poems supplant their cause, are sturdier than trees, and will strip the teeth of any saw that tries to down them.

Both Thoreau and Hopkins in their own ways contest the passing of time by summoning, through the strength of their writing, a kind of eternal present, invoking the "rule that reads: never enter time, and you will never be required to exit." Gass assures us that

> It was lovely to be on Walden Pond at midnight, fluting the fish, but lovelier and more lasting in the verbal than in the fishing lines. It is painful to lose faith even for a moment or see a row of crudely hewn trunks where your favorite rustic scene once was, but mutilation's sorrow is inspiring in the reading, although we realize the poem does not soften the blows felt by the trees.

"The Test of Time," first given as a Woodrow Wilson Lecture, is perhaps a kind of summary statement of Gass's aesthetic philosophy, but it is very much the philosophy that informs Gass's criticism taken as a whole. He is among those few critics who have persisted in defending the aesthetic integrity of literature in an era when literary criticism has increasingly come to regard the aesthetic as an embarrassing frill or an outright impediment to the enlistment of literature in various ideological agendas or in a program of social or moral improvement. Although Gass is a very different kind of critic than Harold Bloom, who is more interested in the psychoanalytic origins of works of literature than in their immediate aesthetic effects, Gass nevertheless shares with Bloom, if not a belief in "literature as a way of life," as Bloom puts it in his most recent book, then certainly a commitment to it as a supreme human achievement and experience. And while Gass perhaps does not quite pursue "an erotics of art," as Susan Sontag called for, his appreciation of both prose and poetry usually emphasizes the pleasure of attentive reading receptive to the sensual qualities of language and the dynamism of the imagination at its most engaged.

Perhaps Gass occupies as a critic a space somewhere between the aesthetic purity of Sontag's notion and the explorations in poetic genealogy performed by Bloom. He doesn't assume that works of literary art will be harmed by efforts to "interpret," as long as such interpretation does justice to the aesthetic integrity of literary art, but his own efforts are focused more on the tangible properties of texts than are Bloom's considerations of the deeper sources of literary creation.

Although Gass's essays are ultimately too voluminous, varied, and too occupied with identifying the value of other works and writers to be regarded as a critical justification of his own fiction, they nevertheless do help us to gain perspective on Gass's fiction, in which he too asks readers to "immerse" themselves in description and detail as revealed through the rhythms of his prose and the vigor of his language. Combining an intensity of style and a preoccupation with form, his fiction always impresses on the reader's attention its arrangements and figurations of language, as Gass's own effort to refuse to "enter Time." In this way the essays perhaps form a mutually reinforcing complement to the fiction, the one adeptly practicing what the others eloquently preach.

Michael Gorra's *Portrait of a Novel* and "In-Between" Criticism

There is no inherent reason why what is called "academic criticism" cannot be of interest to non-academic readers. Certainly the formalist approach of New Criticism, which offers the reader a more focused perspective on the way a work of literature produces its effects, as well as an older-style historical criticism, which offers a view of the work's affiliations with other writing of the period and with the ideas and assumptions characteristic of the period itself, could be of interest to the general reader, although even when these critical methods were ascendant, academic critics were often enough perceived as too far removed from ordinary readers' concerns. Whether or not this perception was in some cases justified, certainly the strategy of "close reading" associated with the New Critics has persisted as a valid critical principle even among general-interest book reviewers, and if current literary culture can't be called rigorous in its adherence to shared critical standards, it does retain at least some residual allegiance to the idea that works of literature, including new works, deserve, and can withstand, some degree of conscientious explication and analysis.

On the other hand, academic criticism in its current form, the form dominant in most academic journals and the most prestigious academic presses, is not likely to be of interest or use to readers interested in how criticism might help to sharpen the reading experience. While academic critics still often profess to be offering a "close reading" of a text, it is usually not a reading intended to illuminate the work in such a way that readers might approach it more fruitfully. Not only is the interest the critic takes in the work likely to be from a narrow perspective centered on politics, history, or social context, but the political considerations won't simply concern the political background of the author or subject, and the historical and social analysis won't primarily situate the work in its time to assist understanding or clarify themes and implicit assumptions, all of which could still contribute to a more informed reading experience. Instead, the political agenda will be the critic's own, as a part of which critical analysis is intended, while historical, social, and cultural forces will themselves be the critic's ultimate focus, not the way these forces shape the aesthetic character of a poem, a novel, or a writer's work as a whole. "Literary theory" may be offered, but there won't be much that's literary about it.

Of course, very little that is actually offered to general readers in book reviews, magazines, or trade publishing could be called academic criticism. Via the latter, the only attention given to literature is through biographies of writers, which in turn become the prompt for what passes as literary criticism in periodicals such as the *New York Review of Books*, noodling essays in which the reviewer makes sweeping statements about a writer's work, often simply repeating the conventional wisdom, while otherwise mostly recapitulating whatever biography is under review. In this context, Michael Gorra's *Portrait of a Novel: Henry James and the Making of an American Masterpiece* is a welcome and potentially important book. The title suggests the book will be a work of criticism elucidating the first of James's "major" novels, *Portrait of a Lady*, but in elucidating the novel Gorra draws on James's life experiences as well, so that the book could be described as criticism informed by biography or as the rare kind of biography that is also credible as literary criticism.

For the most part, Gorra focuses on the years during which James is working on *Portrait*, but he also ranges throughout James's life, considering episodes and events that informed the development of James's sense of himself as a writer, culminating in *Portrait of a Lady*, the book most critics and scholars have long identified as the first truly "Jamesian" of his novels, as well as the direction of James's life and work following *Portrait*, including discussions of his final novels, which in many ways show the techniques and concerns found in the earlier novel extended even more radically and exhaustively. Gorra also chronicles James's relationships with important people in his life, such as brother William and friend Constance Fenimore Woolson, whose romantic feelings for James went unrequited. Gorra judiciously handles the question of James's sexuality, allowing that circumstantial evidence suggests James's sexual desires were likely homoerotic, while also acknowledging there is no actual evidence that he ever acted on those desires (or that he ever acted on any sexual desires at all).

Readers interested in a biography of James should get enough emphasis on the life to satisfy their curiosity, perhaps thus making Gorra's exposition of the genesis of *Portrait of a Lady* and extended analysis of the text itself more palatable, especially as Gorra does about as good a job as it's possible to do in showing how biography can help us at times to appreciate a writer's work. James's experiences as a voluntary exile in Europe can clarify his development of the "international theme," the portrayal of Americans encountering the "old world" of Europe, while learning that *Portrait of a Lady*'s protagonist, Isabel Archer, is in part based on James's "favorite" cousin, Minny Temple, might help explain why he chose to focus on a female protagonist in this first really complex treatment of the theme and perhaps provide insight into the perceived authorial attitude toward Isabel.

Still, Gorra implicitly recognizes the limitations of biographical criticism in making his book not about Henry James but his novel, one which Gorra believes is among the best and most significant novels in American literature. Ultimately his goal is to enhance our appreciation of this novel (and indirectly of Henry James as a fiction writer), in the most old-fashioned sense to account for its greatness. What Gorra has really produced in *Portrait of a Novel* is a work of critical eclecticism. He borrows from a number of critical approaches, including some of those currently ascendant in academic criticism, as well as more traditional "scholarly" concerns, and in the process demonstrates how criticism can draw on a variety of ways of thinking about literature as a phenomenon of human expression and culture in order to satisfy the ultimate goal of providing a clarifying perspective on a morally and aesthetically complex work of literature.

In this way, *Portrait of a Novel* is at least as important for what it represents as a work of criticism as it as a specific commentary on Henry James's novel. Which is not to say the commentary on the novel Gorra provides isn't insightful, in some ways definitive, offering a reading of *Portrait of a Lady* that situates it in its time and place and in its author's body of work, and that explicates its formal and thematic particulars in a style that does justice to the novel's complexity and could appeal to dedicated Jamesians, while also making the analysis accessible to more casual readers of James. In a typically pellucid passage, Gorra considers Isabel's decision to turn down the marriage proposal offered by Lord Warburton:

> When Warburton proposes, Isabel recognizes that she has stepped into a scene she has read too many times before. She may not yet understand just what she wants, but she does recognize that this scene's very familiarity stands in itself as a reason to say no. She rejects the plot that other people might write for her, and insists instead that she must be free to choose, free to make her own mistakes. Her choice here may even be the right one, though that doesn't mean it will lead to happiness. For Isabel cannot escape the fate she seems to crave, the fate that waits to test her in the book's 500 remaining pages. Nor can we. However much we may want to live on in the world of green lawns, we have to recognize that James has made a different and less comfortable plot around this particular woman. . . .

If this account provides insight into Isabel's character, and thus into the "500 remaining pages" of the novel for which she serves as protagonist, it also exemplifies a certain kind of critical discourse, focused on "the text itself," which it is intended to illuminate, but free of acadamese and external agenda, accessible to any serious reader while foregoing the effort to popularize Henry James for a "broader" audience that probably doesn't exist. James is indisputably a sometimes difficult writer (*Portrait of a Lady* somewhat less so than, say, *The Golden Bowl*), and it is a difficulty that astute criticism can help to ameliorate, but James is never going to appeal to all readers, nor does criticism to be worthwhile need to make works of literature equally valuable to all.

Gorra also abstains from personalizing his consideration of *Portrait of a Lady*, from providing "more Gorra" as one reviewer bizarrely wanted him to do. If biography has replaced criticism as the most widely available form of engagement with literature and literary history, the aimlessly subjective focus on the critic's random thoughts and vague impressions has become increasingly more conspicuous in the only remaining form of periodical criticism, the book review. While the emphasis on subjective response is consistent enough with an egocentric American culture, it reduces criticism to the means of recording the critic's idiosyncratic (and often opaque) expressions of "feeling." That Michael Gorra admires *Portrait of a Lady* greatly, that it has had a profound effect on the way he thinks about both life and literature, is perfectly evident, but he translates his personal admiration into a critical language that is descriptive rather than emotional, that registers the novel's palpable effects, not his own intangible fancies.

Our current literary culture could certainly benefit from more books like *Portrait of a Novel*, books that avoid both the intellectual trendiness and abstraction of academic criticism and the undisciplined impressionism of popular criticism. We need popular criticism to be more than biographies overstuffed with trivial details of writers' lives at the expense of greater understanding of their work, an understanding conventional biographies simply can't provide. We need the sort of "in-between" criticism Gorra provides in this book, which could serve as a model for critics who are willing to indulge some of our apparent need for biographical context while keeping the focus on the art the writer made from his/her life. One innovative book does not a trend make, but anyone following up on Gorra's lead would be taking another step toward reviving literary criticism.

David Winters's *Infinite Fictions*

*I*n his introduction to *Infinite Fictions*, his new collection of the reviews he has written over the past several years, David Winters refers to the review as "trivial," even contending that "triviality is among the allures of the form." Of course, Winters surely does not really think his reviews are in fact trivial—if they were, why would he expect anyone to read them, perhaps for some a second time now that they have been bundled together in a book? Instead, his characterization speaks to a no doubt widespread perception that book reviews are utilitarian and ephemeral, good for immediate consumer guidance but without lasting value as literary criticism (to the extent literary criticism itself has lasting value).

Infinite Fictions itself certainly belies the notion that a book review cannot be a credible form of literary criticism. Far from engaging in "trivial" exercises in plot summary or facile judgment, Winters consistently provides meticulous description and analysis, dispensing praise or criticism only while also offering evidence and reasoning to support it. Perhaps in finding the review a congenial form precisely because of its "triviality," Winters is really expressing some impatience with academic criticism, which in its greater length, supposed rigor, and theoretical sophistication is more genuinely serious criticism—"real" criticism—but which in its current incarnation has given up on the job of reckoning with a work's literary qualities per se.

Reckoning with literary qualities is something Winters does exceptionally well. Most of the books discussed in the first section of *Infinite Fictions* ("On Literature") are complex, unconventional works of fiction, and Winters is painstaking in attempting to describe the strategies the author at hand seems to be using, to account for the effect of reading the work as registered in Winters's own experience of it. As he says in the introduction to the book, "As a reviewer, all I can do is try to stay true to the texture of that experience. . .Strange as it sounds, each of these books briefly allowed me to subtract myself from reality. In this respect, when writing reviews, I'm less intent on making prescriptions than on exploring the space left by my subtraction." Thus Winters attends to the specificity of the reading experience itself, something academic criticism generally abjures, while also avoiding the superficial approach of the most "trivial" kind of book reviews, the kind that aim merely to "make prescriptions."

"Subtraction" from reality perhaps seems like a version of being "immersed" in a book, but I would presume Winters means as well something close to what John Dewey called "pure experience," which Dewey believed becomes most accessible to us as aesthetic experience. According to Dewey, aesthetic experience is "experience freed from the forces that impede and confuse its development as experience; freed, that is, from factors that subordinate an experience as it is directly had to something beyond itself." The reader truly receptive to the kind of experience art, in this case literary art, makes available is not in some kind of mystical trance but is fully engaged in an act of what Dewey calls "recreation," perceiving the writer's conceptual and expressive moves thoroughly enough that the reader in effect replays those moves. Literary criticism then becomes in part the attempt to communicate the tenor of this reading experience through the most felicitous description and analytical insight the critic can muster.

I am not suggesting that David Winters is a proponent of the aesthetic philosophy of John Dewey, merely that Winters's account of his reading and reviewing practices seems strikingly evocative of Dewey's theory of "art as experience," which seems to me the most compelling elucidation of both the impulse to create art and the most fruitful way of responding to it. Criticism of fiction, of course, requires first of all an attentiveness to language, and Winters again proves very adept at assessing the stylistic qualities of the fiction he considers. Indeed, he gives special attention throughout the first section of the book to writers associated with the "school of Lish," writers such as Gary Lutz, Sam Lipsyte, Christine Schutt, and Dawn Raffel (not to mention Lish himself), whose work is particularly focused on intricate effects of language. His skill at "close reading" is repeatedly demonstrated in these reviews.

About Lutz's *Divorcer*, Winters observes that "it's as if divorce has seeped into the structure of these 'stories,' like a rot in the grain of their language: something sweetly corrupt that can't be cut out of them. It's buried deep in their syntax, motivating the phrasing that estranges the opening of any errant sentence from its end. In each of the book's seven entries, words are put to work on pulling something apart—a family, a body, a memory of bodies together—in ways that render how life's breaking points really feel when reached." A story by Lipsyte "starts with a sentence setting an initial condition. The second sentence reconfigures the first, curving or swerving back into it. The next sentence swerves harder still, and so on, always with the aim of raising the stakes, tightening the tautness." Dawn Raffel's prose "clings closely to sensory surfaces, calibrating language to the contours of a world which can't clearly be spoken of."

Winters is drawn to fiction in which language does indeed mark a limit, beyond which the real can be sensed or captured fleetingly but otherwise "can't clearly be spoken of." Writing becomes a site where such brief moments of revelation might be afforded, but only through its implicit testimony that the effort to fully grasp a transcendent reality must fail. Thus the reviews in *Infinite Fictions* are focused on works that are not just stylistically but also formally adventurous, fiction that for the most part makes no pretense to be an exercise in realism, since the most realistic fiction would be that which concedes its own impossibility. Several of the books Winters discusses might even be described as subverting literature itself, working to produce a kind of anti-literature, such as Lars Iyers's *Dogma*, which deliberately fails to become literature as "a means of overcoming it," instead becoming "less than literature." Jason Schwartz's *John the Posthumous* is "impossible to synopsize" because it subverts the reading process itself: "In this respect, Schwartz's writing spins the reading process into reverse. His prose puts readers in a position where the most rudimentary aspects of reading are no longer givens . . . ." What Winters says about Gerald Murnane's *Barley Patch* could in some ways apply to most of the fiction he considers. Murnane's novel "begins before literature" in its refusal to take on conventional literary form. It "abandons the prearranged reading paths of realist novels, presenting instead a series of scenes set for stories that forget to occur; it progresses by means of digression and detour."

Winters includes several reviews of translated works, which also proceed through digression and detour, through the avoidance of the usual literary devices that distort rather than illuminate. Appropriately, he does not in these reviews attempt close stylistic analysis (which would at best be misleading for a translated text) but instead emphasizes more plausibly discernible elements such as voice or setting. If these reviews are somewhat more impressionistic, Winters nevertheless conveys a vivid sense of the way these books also participate in the kind of experimentation with form that in its determination to be "less than literature" still manages to extend the possibility of literature. "The book's most unfathomable mystery lies in the way it insistently spells itself out," he writes of Enrique Vila-Matas's *Dublinesque*. "As a result. . .literature is returned to the realm of experience. The novel is not a puzzle to be solved. It has always and already solved itself, bringing what was buried back to life." Similarly, Andrzej Stasiak's *Dukla* is "all surface, all the way down. . .In the end there is no novel, and all that's left is what is sensed and felt."

Part 2 of *Infinite Fictions*, "On Theory," ranges widely over several recent books of literary theory and philosophy, including Terry Eagleton's *The Event of Literature*, Franco Moretti's *Distant Reading*, and Simon Critchley's *The Faith of the Faithless*. Some of the books reviewed are more or less straight theory or philosophy, such as the two books on Heidegger Winters discusses, a book by Jacques Ranciere, and *The Faith of the Faithless*. Others are works of theory as a mode of literary criticism, and, while Winters exhibits a thorough familiarity in general with contemporary critical theory and its philosophical roots, his reviews of the latter books are the most revealing and provide the most continuity with the underlying approach to criticism (and to literature) exemplified in the first part of *Infinite Fictions*.

In his review of Eagleton's book, Winters appears to side with Eagleton in the latter's disapproval of theory's drift from a focus on the specificity of literature to a "culturalism" that, in Winters's words, makes literary criticism "a subfield of cultural studies." Winters describes Eagleton's attempt to renew theory as the attempt "to reassert the centrality of close literary analysis, recovering literature as a determinate object of study." Winters's ultimate lack of enthusiasm for Franco Moretti's quantitative method of "distant reading," the polar opposite of "close literary analysis," is palpable:

> The life that inheres in literature seems too capacious to be captured by a particular critical method. Ironically, many of Moretti's methods rely on instrumental reason—his ideal of distance belongs to the bourgeois spirit. But criticism can't be contained by what any one critic wants of it. Indeed, criticism reveals rhythms of its own, and these are not necessarily those of science.

In his review of Mark M. Freed's *Robert Musil and the Non-modern*, a book that is typical of much contemporary academic criticism in its effort to "apply" critical theory and philosophy to works of literature, Winters perhaps most directly identifies the limitations of theory as a primary mode of literary criticism: "The academic study of literature has reached a slightly strange understanding of itself, if it assumes that insights drawn from philosophy and social theory can straightforwardly account for aspects of fictional worlds, and fictional characters." Winters continues: "Until critics give some closer attention to why they're applying their theories to fictional objects, such applications might seem to rely on little more than a confusion of categories."

Theory can provide a valuable perspective on the implications and entanglements of literature, but it can't subsume it. Winters concludes this review (which really becomes a reflection on the power of Musil's *The Man Without Qualities*) by asserting that "There's something about *The Man Without Qualities* that seems to resist conclusive criticism. Something not so much unfinished as uniquely continuous; infinite. The reason the novel is unlike anything else you've ever read is because it goes on reading itself when you're finished reading it." This "something" is a something not just about this particular novel but all great works of literature. They elude our attempts to find the critical angle that will render them finite, fully fathomed. Criticism can help us begin to fathom what we read, even if a good beginning is all we might really hope for. This book shows David Winters to be a critic remarkably gifted at getting us started.

S.D. Chrostowska's *Matches*

*I*n her book *Literature on Trial* (2012), S. D. Chrostowska examines how the rise of early modern literary criticism is inseparable from the development of literature itself. Forms of criticism, she argues, echoed and adapted emerging literary forms, such that "significant change in the forms (variety, complexity, function) of criticism indicate significant change in the praxis, function, and value of literature, and hence also in literary-critical methods and principles." Although Chrostowska chronicles how certain modes came to be considered more adequate to an authentic critical discourse about literature than others, she also shows how directly the definition of "criticism" tracks the evolving definitions of "literature." (Chrostowska, a professor at York University in Toronto whose scholarly interest focuses loosely on intellectual history and comparative literature, concentrates on the development of criticism in Germany, Poland, and Russia, where the notion of literature as a secular and a vernacular phenomenon developed later than in England and France.)

When in her 2015 book, *Matches*, Chrostowska quotes Paul de Man's reference to literature as a "persistent naming" and then asserts that "The odyssey of naming . . . is at an end," we might find this just another lament about the putative death of literature, but in the context of the author's larger interest in the character of modern literary criticism, it implicitly provides us with an insight into the form and purpose of her book. *Matches* could variously be described as a miscellany, a commonplace book, a series of meditations. Some might initially regard it as a more or less disconnected collection of pensées (a quite sizable collection at that), although the generally abbreviated prose pieces — a few lines to a few pages — that comprise the book are less undeveloped than highly compressed, and what at first seems simply a fragmentary discourse soon enough coheres, structurally and thematically. But certainly readers expecting conventionally realized critical essays, close readings, or historical analyses, the kind of book Chrostowska describes in her introductory "Proem," in which "the words, erect, line up in columns and salute from every page," will have to adjust their assumptions about what "criticism" properly entails.

Chrostowska poses against this sort of text, marshalled in its prescribed formation, one in which words are "laid down in rows, looking up from their cots, sometimes wide, most only half, awake." Lest we think these words are merely slackers, however, they can spring into life quickly: "The words are matches; those that strike ignite. From time to time, light sweeps across the page like wildfire." Obviously, Chrostowska aspires that her book be of the second kind, surely not an unfathomable aspiration, but we could ask whether (or why), in the era when the hegemony of Literature has passed, critical writing such as that found in *Matches* is more sharply attuned to the changes evident in literature and literary culture, better situated to register the reshaping of literary writing in a networked world in which print has been supplanted by pixels. If modern literary criticism originated in a reciprocal relationship with literature as the latter acquires (and attempts to maintain) its conceptual coherence, when that coherence can no longer be taken for granted, does the "odyssey of naming" that is also criticism come to its functional end, or find a different kind of coherence?

Literature on Trial reminds us that the historical interdependence of literature and criticism was thoroughgoing enough that "literature" (as opposed to what previously would simply have been called "poetry") itself came into being as in part an effect of critical discourse. It could be argued, for example, that at least as important to the ultimate acceptance of the novel as a "serious" literary form as was its acceptance by such writers as Flaubert, James, or George Eliot was the effort made on its behalf by reviewers and critics, to the point that in the 20th century the novel became more or less synonymous with "literature" for many readers. Literature is not whatever readers at a certain time declare it to be—not until some process of critical reflection, rooted in the inherited history of similar such reflection, leads them there.

In the 20th century, of course, criticism's authority was only made more explicit by the rise of academic criticism along with the spread of the formal study of vernacular literature in colleges and universities. *Matches* poses its greatest challenge to academic criticism, demonstrating that intellectually rigorous issues can be addressed in an accessible way without diluting or oversimplifying those issues. Chrostowska, an academic critic herself (and also a novelist, the author of the 2009 novel, *Permission*), replaces argument with aphoristic insight, rhetorical elaboration with concise analysis, a tone of earnest formality with wit and irony. Although many passages could be quoted in their entirety as illustration of Chrostowska's approach, this one, headed "Art (Theory) Brut" is representative:

> Caves containing prehistoric art have opened our eyes not just to the oldest known artwork, but to the Urbild of art: the outline of a human hand in ochre done by firelight. From it leads the long and dark passage to the image as we know it: from this negative of a hand held against a wall, on past the contour of an invisible hand and its silhouette, all the way down (or up) to the articulated figure bursting in colour in broadest daylight. But the primitive stencil, followed by the application of the hand to depiction, followed by the pictorial trace of what's behind the depicting and tracing—these were, respectively, the view, the technique, and the principle of art from the very beginning.

The deliberate compression of a fragment such as this lends it a kind of oracular quality that is no doubt too transparently subjective to seem altogether "scholarly," but while of course it can be read in isolation, each fragment interpreted in succession, the book doesn't finally offer such bite-sized chunks of "meaning." Instead it links its fragments and mini-essays in strands of thematic rumination, its subjects, once introduced, examined from complementary angles for a few pages before blending into a new subject, usually related, in a very fluid way that gives *Matches* a theme and variations structure, although many of the themes recur throughout the book, according to changes in context and emphasis.

"Art (Theory) Brut" thus appears as part of a series of entries contemplating the nature and role of art, although the section in which it appears begins with reflections on reading and literature and ultimately considers music and film as well. Similarly, the book's second section maintains a loose focus on philosophy while weaving in meditations on multifarious issues related to philosophical thinking, as does the section following on topics relevant to political thought. Even while *Matches* asks us to direct our attention to its sentences as they are "laid down in rows," this does not mean it can't also be satisfying as a formally adventurous whole. If it is not a text lined up in columns, marching forward to its appointed rhetorical unity, nevertheless the associations among the subjects Chrostowska treats, across all six sections of the book, are certainly evident enough to make it a "text" in the first place, not a series of random observations.

Matches is not a wholly unprecedented book, of course. In particular, writers such as Schlegel, Nietzsche, Walter Benjamin, and Maurice Blanchot created aphoristic, fragmented, and/or unorthodox works of literary criticism that have been very influential, retaining their intellectual credibility while not classifiable as "academic" per se. In following up on the efforts of such writers, Chrostowska seems implicitly to be contending that the potential of the critical miniature has not been fully realized. However large figures such as Nietzsche and Benjamin loom in modern criticism, it is their ideas that have compelled attention, not the forms in which those ideas were cast, and Chrostowska's book prompts us to consider the extent to which the ideas proffered by these influential thinkers were conditioned by their mode of presentation. In *Matches*, the entries that most call attention to their own mediation through form are perhaps those composed of dialogues between "A" and "B" (in a few cases "Q" and "A"). This form inherently puts authorial intent in suspension (is the author A or B?); it seems likely that Chrostowska the novelist has some influence on Chrostowska the critic's sense of the potentially permeable boundaries between literature and criticism, although *Literature on Trial* reminds us that this potential has been exploited in criticism all along.

Chrostowska herself exploits it not just in *Matches* but in her novel *Permission* as well. A version of an epistolary novel (except that the only correspondent is the novel's protagonist), structured as a series of emails, the novel ultimately has a story to tell (including the story of its own creation), but in part it is an opportunity for its protagonist to discourse on subjects such as Montaigne and the films of Stan Brakhage, the reality of death and the ritual wooden masks of Pacific Northwest Indians, in some ways not unlike the strategy employed in *Matches*. Indeed, it would not be wholly implausible to regard *Matches* as itself a novel of sorts, its authorial voice belonging to a character occupied with the same kind of concerns explored by the narrator of *Permission*. Ultimately, however, the book covers such a wide range of subjects and is sufficiently reticent about asserting a "thesis" or in some way personalizing the text that, if it is appropriate to call *Permission* a novel that pursues an essayistic strategy, probably it is most accurate to consider *Matches* a work of critical nonfiction written by an author displaying a decidedly "literary" sensibility.

Perhaps it would be most fruitful to think of *Matches* in the context of this aphorism expressed early in the book: "Now that you have lost your faith in Literature—it does nothing for your *amour propre* these days—you can believe in writing." Capital-l Literature—the ultimate product of the dialectic between criticism and the forms of what we now think of as literature—imposes a conceptual abstraction, one fraught with issues of reputation and cultural authority, on the aesthetic integrity of "writing" unencumbered by extraneous expectations or ambitions. That we no longer believe in the exalted status of Literature frees the writer to "believe in writing" anew. *Matches* suggests it can free the critic as well: the academic or scholarly critic can dispense with the burdensome apparatus of citation and elaboration associated with the scholarly article; the book reviewer or general interest literary critic presumably could seek an alternative to the conventional evaluative review or critical essay.

Should literary critics want such an alternative? Certainly *Matches* demonstrates that an intelligent, informed critic can use the aphorism and the fragment to explore the most serious and substantive critical and philosophical subjects, providing sufficiently radiant illumination to guide us in our own consideration of these subjects. It is a very rewarding book, read either in sequence and in its entirety or in isolated selections, but while Chrostowska has written in *Matches* a refreshing, consistently thoughtful work that usefully questions entrenched assumptions about the nature of criticism, it is less a specific model of what criticism might become in the digital age than simply a challenge to seriously reflect on what Matthew Arnold called "the function of criticism at the present time." That function is not the function Arnold advocated for his time, since we no longer believe in such a thing as a "disinterested" perspective. Still, it could be argued that if faith in Literature is to be replaced with trust in writing, criticism could have an even more important function in helping to reconcile confused readers to this real death of literature. Finally this requires critics who come to realize that the passing of Literature and its metaphysical demands allows us to see that a very corporeal writing can then come to life.

Bibliography

Bibliography

Bloom, Harold. *The Anatomy of Influence: Literature as a Way of Life.* New Haven: Yale University Press, 2011.

———. *The Anxiety of Influence: A Theory of Poetry.* New York: Oxford University Press, 1973.

Carey, John. *What Good Are the Arts?* New York: Oxford University Press, 2005.

Chrostowska, S.D. *Literature on Trial: The Emergence of Critical Discourse in Germany, Poland and Russia, 1700-1800.* Toronto: University of Toronto Press, 2012.

———. *Matches: A Light Book.* New York: Punctum Books, 2015.

Conte, Joseph M. *Design and Debris: A Chaotics of Postmodern American Fiction.* Tuscaloosa: University of Alabama Press, 2002.

Dewey, John. *Art as Experience.* New York: Perigree Books, 1934.

Dickstein, Morris. *Dancing in the Dark: A Cultural History of the Great Depression.* New York: W.W. Norton & Company, 2010.

———. *Gates of Eden: American Culture in the Sixties.* New York: Basic Books, 1977.

———. *Leopards in the Temple: The Transformation of American Fiction, 1945-70.* Cambridge, MA.: Harvard University Press, 2002.

———. *Mirror in the Roadway: Literature and the Real World.* Princeton, N.J.: Princeton University Press, 2005.

BIBLIOGRAPHY

Drucker, Johanna. *Sweet Dreams: Contemporary Art and Complicity*. Chicago: University of Chicago Press, 2005.

Flood, Alison. "Books Bloggers Are Harming Literature, Warns Booker Prize Head Judge." *The Guardian* 25 Sep. 2010.

Franzen, Jonathan. "Mr. Difficult." *The New Yorker* 30 Sep. 2002.

Gass, William H. "The Test of Time." *Tests of Time: Essays*. New York: Knopf, 2002.

Gorra, Michael. *Portrait of a Novel: Henry James and the Making of an American Masterpiece*. New York: Liveright, 2013.

Hitchens, Christopher. *Love, Poverty, and War: Journeys and Essays*. New York: Nation Books, 2004.

———. *Unacknowledged Legislation: Writers in the Public Sphere*. London: Verso, 2000.

———. *Why Orwell Matters*. New York: Basic Books, 2002.

Kostelanatz, Richard. *The End of Intelligent Writing: Literary Politics in America*. New York: Sheed and Ward, 1974.

Mendelson, Daniel. "A Critic's Manifesto." *The New Yorker* 28 Aug. 2012.

———. "The Collector." *The New Republic* 14 April, 2009.

Parker, Hershel. *Flawed Texts and Verbal Icons: Literary Authority in American Fiction*. Evanston, Ill.: Northwestern University Press, 1984.

———. *Melville Biography: An Inside Narrative*. Evanston, Ill.: Northwestern University Press, 2012.

Poirier, Richard. *Poetry and Pragmatism*. Cambridge, MA: Harvard University Press, 1992.

———. *The Renewal of Literature: Emersonian Reflections*. New York: Random House, 1987.

———. *A World Elsewhere: The Place of Style in American Literature*. New York: Oxford University Press, 1966.

Silliman, Ron. *The New Sentence*. New York: Roof Books, 1987.

Sontag, Susan. *Against Interpretation*. 1966. New York: Octagon Books, 1978.

Winters, David. *Infinite Fictions*. Winchester, UK: Zero Books, 2015.

Wood, James. *The Fun Stuff*. New York: Farrar, Straus, and Giroux, 2012.

———. *How Fiction Works*. New York: Farrar, Straus, and Giroux, 2008.

———. *The Irresponsible Self: On Laughter and the Novel*. New York: Picador, 2005.

Acknowledgments

Acknowledgments

Thanks to the following publications, where earlier versions of some of these essays originally appeared:

"Life on the Page: How the Fiction James Wood Really Likes Works" (in *Open Letters Monthly*)

"'The Thoughts of Other People': James Wood and the Realism of 'Mind'" (in *The Quarterly Conversation*)

"Legislating: Christopher Hitchens as Literary Critic" (in *Agni Online*)

"On Harold Bloom" (in *The Quarterly Conversation*)

"Acts of Rendition" (On Richard Poirier) (in *Open Letters Monthly*)

"Looked at Importantly" (in *The Big Other*—Birthday Tribute to William Gass)

"A Flare for Criticism" (in *Los Angeles Review of Books*)

www.ingramcontent.com/pod-product-compliance
Lightning Source LLC
Chambersburg PA
CBHW020617300426
44113CB00007B/682